GETTING STARTED

100 Icebreakers
for Youth Gatherings

Patty Hupfer Riedel

Hi-Time✳Pflaum

Dayton, OH 45449

Getting Started
100 Icebreakers for Youth Gatherings
Patty Hupfer Riedel

Interior Design by Carole Ohl, P.S. Creative Group
Cover Design by Linda Becker

ISBN 0-937997-59-5

Contents

Contents

Introduction

Active Learning

I teach chemistry, and I want my students to feel comfortable enough to ask questions of me or of anyone else in the class. Chemistry is a tough subject. If you are afraid to reach out for help, you can have a pretty tough time. That is why I build in experiential, or active, learning experiences, through which group members learn by taking part in games, role playing, problem solving, debates, competitions, and communications. Icebreakers help people get to know one another, relax, laugh, and feel part of a team. This process of getting acquainted and team building is important in church groups, school groups, corporate meetings—and chemistry classes. It is necessary for all age groups.

Active Learning—in a non-threatening way— has a number of advantages.
- The time spent together in a group helps form relationships or make established relationships stronger. That's the priority.
- Participants enjoy being involved. It's not the old "sit down, be quiet, and listen" format. Group members interact, ask questions, and laugh a lot.
- It encourages creativity, promotes thoughts and ideas. Group members aren't told the answers. They find the answers.
- It provides a safe place to make mistakes and learn from them.

How to Use This Book

The activities in this book are pretty straightforward. Most need no supplies, and the rest need very few. All activities have been tested, and they work. Of course, you are the best judge for deciding if a particular activity is appropriate for your group.

The activities are divided into three categories: Getting Acquainted, Thought Provokers, and Energizers. Within each group, the activities are arranged alphabetically by title. If there is any worksheet needed for an activity, it is provided in the Appendix, and you are permitted to copy that page.

Most activities would fit into any of the three categories, but to provide the best structure for the book, I decided on these definitions for the categories: • **Getting Acquainted** activities are very non-threatening ways to get your group participants to know one another. • **Thought Provokers** get participants to know one another on a deeper level. • **Energizers** are lively experiences that fill the group members with energy and spur them to work together in various situations.

Read the rules of each activity more than once before using it so that you feel comfortable with it. Some activities are done just for fun, but many can be processed or discussed at the end, which is often the best part of the whole exercise. I'm continually amazed at what each group gets out of the various activities, and how the same activity can spark different reactions from different groups.

I did not set an age range for each activity. With a few adaptations, I believe they work with any age. I've used them for age groups that range from middle-schoolers through adults. From my own use of these activities, I know that your groups will benefit from them. And I also know that you will as well. Just don't forget to bring your own enthusiasm, openness, and energy to every group gathering. Now jump in and enjoy!

Dedication

To Anne Hupfer Stevenson,
        my role model and guide
        as I've followed in her footsteps so many times.

And to Don Larsen and Earl Reum,
        for inspiration and the chances to lead.

BACK-TO-BACK, PEOPLE-TO-PEOPLE

Purpose: Gives participants a high-energy mixer game in which to interact with a large number of people.

Group Size: 25 to unlimited

Time: 15 minutes

Supplies: None

Directions:

1. Everyone should have a partner except the person who is *It*. If the partners don't know each other, they should introduce themselves.
2. *It* calls out directions such as "back to back," "shoulder to shoulder," "foot to knee," "hand to head," "head to head," and so on.
3. Partners must position their bodies in the manner directed by *It*.
4. When *It* calls out "People to People," everyone—including *It*—must find a new partner.
5. The one person left without a partner is the new *It*, who then calls out a new set of positions to take.
6. Make sure *It* keeps the directions flowing in order to give the game a high energy pace.
7. When partners change, remind them to introduce themselves if they don't know each other.

BALLOON QUESTIONS

Purpose: Because you make up the questions beforehand, you can either stick to a particular theme or make this a general getting-to-know-you activity.

Group Size: 10 - 30

Time: 15 - 30 minutes

Supplies: One balloon for each person; the balloons should have questions already tucked inside of them (for starters, see suggested questions on Appendix pages 83 and 84, "Boundary Breaking Questions").

Directions:

1. Give each person a non-inflated balloon with a question rolled up and tucked inside. (Balloons are not inflated to save you time, but if you want to inflate them beforehand, that's okay too.)
2. Participants blow up their balloons and tie them shut.
3. On the count of three, everyone tosses the balloon into the air. The group has to keep all balloons in the air for 1 minute in order to get the balloons mixed up. This also gives the group something active to do before they sit down to answer the questions.
4. When you say "stop," everyone should grab a balloon and hold onto it.
5. Ask for a volunteer. Instruct the volunteer to pick someone to help pop his or her balloon.
6. After the balloon is popped, the person reads the question and answers it. The one who helped pop the balloon goes next, choosing someone else to assist him or her.
7. Having someone help pop the balloon keeps a flow to the order for who goes next. Another advantage to having a helper is that some people don't like popping balloons, and it's nice to have moral support.

BIRTHDAYS

Purpose: Divides a large group into smaller groups while discovering some common ground among group members.

Group Size: Unlimited (the bigger the better)

Time: 15 - 30 minutes

Supplies: None

Directions:

1. Tell everyone to find all the other people in the room who have the same birth month. (It can get loud at this point!)

2. When it seems that most people have found their groups, call out "Where are all the Januaries?" (Continue with each month of the year until you have all the months that are represented.) Do this to make sure all the groups are together and not fragmented.

3. Instruct each group to make up a cheer, song, or saying (15–30 seconds long) that represents their birth month. Allow no more than five minutes for this.

4. Have each group present the results of their creativity.

CHECKERBOARD CHALLENGE

Purpose: Encourages problem solving, team communication, and strategizing.

Group Size: 6 – 12

Time: 10 minutes, plus discussion

Supplies: Masking tape to make the checkerboard on the floor—or a checkerboard pattern taped on a tarp that can be used over and over again.

Directions:

1. Show the group the checkerboard pattern. Tell them that there is a secret path that enables them to cross the checkerboard. The problem is only you know the secret path. Participants have to find the path by trial and error, with each person in turn trying to step on the correct sequence of squares. Explain that the choices for correct squares will always be forward, diagonally forward, or sideways.

2. Since no one can talk or communicate in any way once the game begins, some planning has to take place ahead of time and everyone must be paying attention. Allow a few minutes for planning strategies and for the team to decide in what order each member will go.

3. Only one person can be on the board at a time, and each player must have a turn before anyone tries a second time.

4. The first person in line steps on a square. If it is an incorrect square, you "buzz" the move, and the player goes to the end of the line. If it is the correct square, the player may try another square.

5. As each player's turn comes, he or she should know which squares have been buzzed and which haven't, if the player has been paying attention.

6. A player's turn continues until he or she steps on an incorrect square. The object is to get the whole team across the board using the correct squares.

7. You should have a few patterns already drawn out that you will allow the group to follow without being buzzed. A couple of samples are below, but you can work out others if you wish.

8. After the game is ended, process the activity:
   • What was frustrating about the rules and why?
   • What was good about the rules and why?
   • If you could play again, would you change anything?
   • What is important about choosing the right strategy?
   • How could you relate what you learned to real life problems?

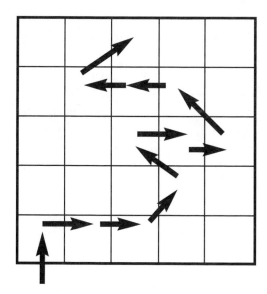
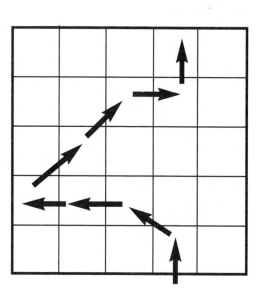

COLORED CANDIES GAME

Purpose: Provides a fun (and tasty) way to get to know others. After assessing your group and deciding on your goal for this activity, you can establish the depth of the sharing by the categories you establish.

Group Size: 5 – 20

Time: 20 – 40 minutes

Supplies: One fun-size pack of assorted colored candies for every group member. (Make sure no one has a food allergy, e.g., nuts or chocolate.)

Directions:

1. Arrange group members in a circle and give each person a fun-size pack of candies.
2. Each person should open their pack and group their candies by color. Each color of candy represents a different topic. The number of candies a player has of a certain color determines the number of responses they have to share with the group. For instance, if Player A has three red candies, he or she should name three hobbies. If Player B has one red candy, he or she names one hobby.
3. The following categories are just suggestions. Make up ones that fit your group, or ask more specific ones if you prefer. Adjust the colors for the candy you use.
   - Red – hobbies you have or would like to have
   - Blue – things about your family that they wouldn't mind your sharing
   - Yellow – things about yourself that you are proud of
   - Green – places you've traveled to
   - Brown – things you'd like to do in the next ten years
   - Orange – goals for your church group this year (school groups, sports teams, families, etc.)
4. Have everyone respond to the same color as you take turns around the circle. When all the reds have been answered, then move on to the next color.
5. Don't forget to eat the candy as you go along!

COMIC STRIP LINEUP

Purpose: Helps split a large group into smaller groups and encourages working together to solve a problem. It's also good for a lot of laughs.

Group Size: 15 - 100

Time: 10 minutes

Supplies: Comic strips cut into single panels; masking tape.

Directions:

1. Give each group member a comic strip panel and a piece of masking tape. Have them tape their panel to their shirt front.
2. Everyone has to walk around and find the others who have the same comic strip.
3. Once they all find one another, they should arrange themselves in the correct order for the comic strip to make sense.
4. When all the groups are done, have each completed strip come to the front of the room, identify themselves by the comic strip they represent, and read themselves aloud.

DO YOU LIKE YOUR NEIGHBOR?

Purpose: Provides practice in remembering names while learning a little more about other group members.

Group Size: 15 – 30

Time: 15 – 30 minutes

Supplies: One sturdy chair for each participant except the one leading the group.

Directions:

1. Everyone should sit in a circle with the leader in the middle of the group.

2. The leader steps in front of one of the group members and asks, "[Name], do you like your neighbor?"

3. The responding person, using the names of the people on his or her left and right, says, "Yes, I like my neighbors [Name] and [Name]." Continuing, the responder says, "But I *really* like people who...." The responder should complete the sentence with something that will get the others to change places. For instance:

   ...have birthdays in July and August

   ...saw *The Lion King*

   ...is wearing athletic shoes (name a brand to be more selective)

   ...has pierced ears

   ...has a little brother

4. Anyone who fits into the category mentioned must stand up and trade places with others who fit into the same category. During the exchange of places, the leader tries to get a seat. The person left standing is the new leader.

5. If you like, another rule can be added. The leader asks the question, "Do you like your neighbor?" The person asked can respond "No!" At that point, all group members must change places.

6. Game continues for as long as you want it to.

DROP A SHEET

Purpose: Helps people learn the names of participants and explores reactions to being "on the spot."

Group Size: 15 – 30

Time: 10 minutes

Supplies: Sheet, blanket, or tarp (something you can't see through).

Directions:

1. Divide group into two even teams. You also need two sheet holders. (You can be one of them, if you wish.)
2. The sheet, which will serve as a wall, is held up as high as it can be while still touching the floor.
3. The teams sit on either side of the sheet so that they cannot see each other.
4. Each group secretly selects one person to walk up to within a foot of the sheet. On the count of three, the sheet holders lower the sheet.
5. The first of the two people at the sheet to shout out the other's name correctly wins that round and gets a point for the team.
6. Continue the process with two new people at the sheet. The winning team is the one with the most points when the time is up.
7. Process the activity by asking:
   - Why might you want to or not want to face another person when the sheet is dropped?
   - What makes this game easy or hard?
   - Why are some people better at this game than others?
   - What does pressure do to your focus?

Note: Avoid setting up so that windows, mirrors, or TV screens might reflect the other side of the sheet. You don't want anyone cheating, do you?

FAMOUS PEOPLE

Purpose: Gives participants a fun, relaxed way of mixing without having to reveal "personal" information.

Group Size: 10 – 50

Time: 10 minutes

Supplies: Adhesive nametag for each participant; make the nametags from slips of paper with a loop of masking tape on one side.

Directions:

1. On each nametag or slip of paper write the name of a famous person, living or dead.
2. Attach a nametag to each person's back.
3. Each group member has to figure out whose name is on his or her back by asking other participants only questions that can be answered "yes" or "no." (Is this person a female/male? Is she in the entertainment business? Was he alive in this century? Did she ever do voices for cartoon characters?)
4. Play until everyone has figured out what famous person's name is on their back.

FIND YOUR MATE

Purpose: Helps form pairs out of a large group and provides practice in solving problems.

Group Size: Unlimited

Time: 20 minutes

Supplies: For each participant, prepare an index card or small sheet of paper by writing the name of one of a famous pair (see samples below); strips of adhesive or masking tape.

Directions:

1. Tape a card or paper to each person's back.
2. Explain that everyone must first figure out what or who is written on their tag and then find their other half.
3. Participants must limit their questions to those that can be answered "yes" or "no," and they can ask only three questions of the same person. After three questions are asked, they must move on to another person.
4. Continue with the game until everyone is paired up.
5. At this point, you can conclude the activity or begin another activity that needs paired participants.

Variation: A quick change in this activity is to have everyone wear their tags on their front sides. This way they know what/who they are and can just look for their partner. This works faster and is especially good for younger people or very large groups.

Sample Pairs

Peanut butter/Jelly	Peas/Carrots
Macaroni/Cheese	Tweedle Dee/Tweedle Dum
R2D2/C3PO	Black/White
Charlie Brown/Snoopy	Table/Chair
Fred Astaire/Ginger Rogers	Dorothy/Toto
Santa Claus/Ho Ho Ho	Batman/Robin

GOTCHA!

Purpose: Establishes a fun structure for meeting others and learning their names plus a little additional information about them.

Group Size: 25 – unlimited. The more the better!

Time: 10 minutes

Supplies: GOTCHA! Activity Sheet for each participant (see Appendix page 85); pen or pencil for each participant.

Directions:

1. Everyone should have a copy of the GOTCHA! Activity Sheet and a pen or pencil.
2. Each person has ten minutes to accomplish everything on the sheet and to get the required signatures.

GROUP JUGGLE-TOSS

Purpose: Gets everyone in the group involved and keeps them active. This multi-purpose activity offers practice in listening, learning names, focusing, communication, and organization.

Group Size: 10 – 30

Time: 10 – 15 minutes

Supplies: A variety of balls or other objects to toss (examples: tennis ball, bean bag, squeaky toy, rubber chicken, soft frisbee, rubber ball, raw or hard boiled egg).

Directions:

1. Group members stand in a circle.

2. Tell the group, "We are going to toss the ball in a set pattern so that each person receives the ball once. I'm always going to toss the ball to [Name], who will then toss it to [Name], who tosses it on to [Name]." Continue setting the pattern until everyone's name has been called out. Explain that the last person should toss it back to you (or another leader, if you prefer).

3. Practice tossing one of the objects through one cycle of the pattern to make sure it is set in everyone's mind.

4. Instruct the group to say aloud the name of the person to whom they are tossing the object. This helps get the other person's attention and also helps people remember the names of others in the group.

5. Start by throwing one of the objects, then begin adding the other objects so that there are multiple objects going around the group at one time.

6. Continue until all the balls/objects get back to you.

7. Process the activity the way that enforces your desired outcome. Here are some sample questions:

   • What can we learn from this activity?

   • How can you relate this to organization (communication, listening skills)?

   • Which object was the easiest/most difficult to catch? Why? (Sometimes we're more careful with certain objects. That's also true about certain information with which we are entrusted. Discuss types of information people receive and what they do with that information.)

   • Why is it important to use someone's name?

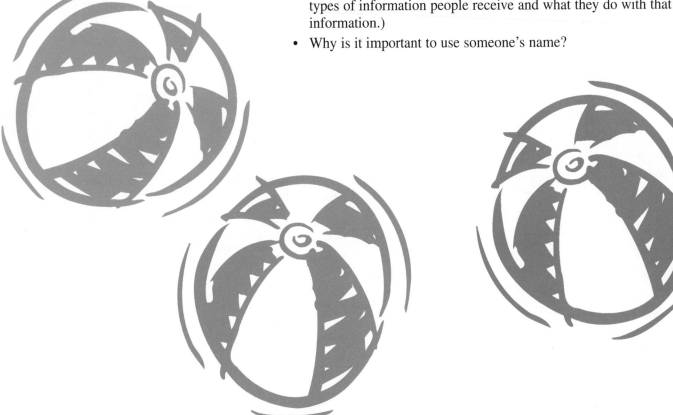

HOT BEACH BALL

Purpose: Provides a hands-on activity that combines movement with questions and helps everyone learn bits and pieces about the others.

Group Size: 10 – 30

Time: 15 minutes

Supplies: Beach ball or other large ball.

Directions:

1. The group stands in a circle with a little distance between them.

2. Begin by asking a question and tossing the ball to another person. That person must answer the question and toss the ball to a new person, who answers the question and tosses the ball to another person. The ball gets tossed until everyone has answered the question. No one answers the same question twice.

3. The object is to keep the ball moving so no one is holding it more than three seconds. The questions have to be simple and not too in-depth.

4. To help keep things moving, have the participants hold their hands up if they haven't had the ball yet and put them at their side once they've received the ball and answered the question.

5. Here are some sample questions:
   - What is your favorite color?
   - Name a book you've read.
   - Who is your favorite cartoon character?
   - What is a word beginning with G?
   - What is your favorite fruit?
   - Name the song you last heard.
   - What sport do you like to play?
   - What is a good movie to watch?
   - What is your favorite ice cream flavor?
   - What is your favorite season?

HUMAN TREASURE HUNT

Purpose: Forms and re-forms many different groups of people in a short amount of time, providing an opportunity to get acquainted as quickly as possible.

Group Size: 25 – unlimited

Time: 5 – 10 minutes

Supplies: Whistle or microphone, depending on availability.

Directions:

1. All participants should be in one large room or area.

2. You will be calling out various ways to organize into groups, and the participants are to follow your directions each time—probably changing groups with each new direction. The idea is to get in as many groups as possible in a short amount of time.

3. If it is a very large group, use a microphone if possible. Otherwise, blow a whistle each time a new formation is to be called out so that people will listen to the new direction.

4. Here are some ideas… make more up as you go along.

   - Find someone with the same size thumb as you.
   - Find two people whom you don't know at all.
   - Find one person with the same birth month as you.
   - Find three people whose favorite subject is different from yours.
   - Find two people who live twenty or more miles from you.
   - Find one person who likes the same sport as you.
   - Find four people who are wearing at least one item of clothing that is the same color as yours.
   - Find two people who have different brands or types of shoes than you.

"IT GIVES ME GREAT PLEASURE TO INTRODUCE..."

Purpose: Get to know at least one person fairly well and then introduce that person to the rest of the group.

Group Size: 6 – 20 (or unlimited if you want to skip the large-group introductions)

Time: 10 minutes per pair to fill out sheet. 2 minutes per person to read sheet.

Supplies: For each participant, an "It Gives Me Great Pleasure to Introduce…" worksheet (see Appendix page 88) and a pen or pencil.

Directions:

1. Divide the group into pairs (see Getting into Groups, page 58, for suggestions). If you have an uneven number in the large group, have one group of three people.

2. Distribute the worksheets. Allow ten minutes for the participants to fill in the information about their partners.

3. If time allows, have participants introduce their partners to the rest of the group. If there is not time for this, then at least two people got to know each other better.

THE MALL GAME

Purpose: Helps group members learn one another's names in a fast, fun, and effective way.

Group Size: 10 – 30

Time: 20 – 30 minutes

Supplies: None

Directions:

1. Ask the group to sit in a circle.
2. Tell everyone to imagine that they are shopping in a gigantic mall—a mall that has *EVERYTHING*! Each person needs to buy one item that begins with the first letter of his or her first name. Once everyone has "found" their item the game begins.
3. Start by saying your own first name and the item you bought. For instance, I might say, "Patty Popcorn Popper." A variation is to add an action while stating your name and item. I could wiggle all my fingers in the air while saying, "Patty Popcorn Popper." (Try to discourage actions that involve standing up or moving out of the circle.)
4. In turn, each person says his or her name and item and repeats the previous person's information. So, the second person would say "Jim Jack-in-the-Box, Patty Popcorn Popper."
5. Continue clockwise around the circle with everyone saying their name and item and repeating all the previous information.
6. Since the first few people in the circle have fewer names and items to remember and the last few people in the circle don't have their names repeated very often, you may want to go around the circle again and have each person repeat all the names and items one last time.
7. Remember that it is always okay to help people out if they forget any part of the information. We don't want to embarrass anyone. We want to learn names.

Variation

If the group is really large, you may want to require that only the previous seven names be repeated.

NAMETAG

Purpose: Helps group members learn more about one another and reflect on areas of common ground.

Group Size: Unlimited

Time: 15 minutes

Supplies: 8 ½" x 11" paper for each participant; markers; loops of tape.

Directions:

1. Have everyone in the group make an oversized name tag with the following information on it: first and last name, favorite color, favorite subject, favorite movie, and dream vacation. Encourage them to use the whole sheet of paper and set it up on the horizontal with their first names most prominent. See sample below.

2. After everyone has taped their name tag on their chests, have them mingle around the room and read one another's tags. But, they cannot speak to anyone unless they have something in common on their tags.

3. If they have something in common, they can talk about anything on the name tag. If nothing is in common, they can only read the tag and absorb the information without comment.

4. Process the activity with questions like the following:
   - What did you find out about others?
   - How did it feel when you found something in common with someone else?
   - How did it feel when you couldn't talk with certain people?

Favorite Color		Favorite Subject
	First Name	
	Last Name	
Dream Vacation		Favorite Movie

PEOPLE BINGO

Purpose: Helps group mix and ask questions of one another.

Group Size: 12 – unlimited

Time: 10 minutes

Supplies: People Bingo Worksheet (see Appendix page 89) and pen or pencil for each participant.

Directions:

1. Give each participant a People Bingo Worksheet and make sure they have a pen or pencil.
2. Instruct everyone to mingle, find a person who fits each description on the worksheet, and have that person sign the appropriate square.
3. One person can sign another's paper only once.
4. Allow enough time so almost everyone gets their sheet filled up.
5. At the end, ask the group, "Whose name did you put down for Can Juggle?" The group will shout out a few names. Ask those persons to come to the front and demonstrate with wads of paper. The same can be done for telling a joke, singing "Row, Row, Row Your Boat," and demonstrating CPR. (Avoid any demonstration of something that might result in injury, such as doing cartwheels.)

PICTURE PROVERBS

Purpose: Uses visual clues for a guessing game about well known proverbs. This activity can be done as a competition between two teams or as whole-group activity.

Group Size: 10 – 25

Time: 15 minutes

Supplies: Proverbs cut apart into slips and folded (see Appendix page 91); paper and markers or chalkboard and chalk; watch or clock with a sweep hand.

Directions:

1. Put the folded slips of proverbs into a hat or another container.
2. Divide the group into two teams.
3. Team A selects someone to draw the first proverb. He or she picks a proverb and begins drawing. No written words from the proverb may appear in the drawing, only pictures representing the words.
4. Time how long it takes Team A to guess the proverb. Record the number of seconds.
5. Team B selects a representative from their team who picks a proverb and draws it. Record the time it takes Team B to guess the answer.
6. The turn goes back to Team A, who selects a second person to draw. Continue alternating teams until all the proverbs are used.
7. The team with the lowest time score is the winner.

Variation

Do the activity without the competition. Select the appropriate number of group members to draw the proverbs and let everyone guess together. Demonstrate that you don't have to be an artist to get your ideas across.

SANDWICH COOKIE SOLUTIONS

Purpose: Stresses the importance of planning, organizing, and working together.

Group Size: 10 – 50, divided into small groups of 5 or 6 (see Getting into Groups, page 58 for suggestions)

Time: 20 – 45 minutes

Supplies: One package of sandwich cookies for each group, or other "Building Supplies" (see suggestions below).

Directions:

1. Divide the large group into teams of five or six people. Keeping the teams small gives everyone a chance to be involved.

2. Decide ahead of time what the goal of this activity will be. Some ideas are to build the tallest structure...the most creative structure...to use the white filling in the most unusual way...to create a machine that will solve one of the world's worst problems.

3. Give the groups about five minutes to plan before you distribute the supplies. (Otherwise they set right to work before planning what they want to do.)

4. Allow ten to twenty minutes for the groups to finish their creations.

5. Have each group present and explain their creation to the large group.

6. You can judge who did the best job of reaching the goal, or let the groups vote.

7. Process the activity when you are done.

   - Did your creation turn out the way you planned it at the beginning?
   - How did you come up with your idea?
   - What were some, if any, difficulties you encountered?
   - Would you do this activity differently next time? How?
   - Were you happy with the outcome?
   - What is the advantage of planning the activity before you begin?
   - Did you all agree about what the outcome was to be?
   - How can you relate this to things you do every day?

Other Building Supplies

- straws and tape
- graham crackers and frosting
- newspaper and tape
- things found in the recycling bin (various paper and cardboard)
- different types of pasta
- marshmallows and toothpicks
- a bag of supplies you give each team (10 paper clips, 10 index cards, 2 milk jugs, strips of construction paper, a yard of masking tape, 15 spaghetti noodles, etc.)

SEND ME YOUR CHAMPION

Purpose: Provides a team competition activity in which the whole group must get involved or the champion can't be created. Lots of spirited competition.

Group Size: At least three teams of 15 – 30 on each

Time: 15 minutes

Supplies: Qualifications list (See below for starters, and then add your own if you wish.)

Directions:

1. Have each group huddle together to be ready to create their champion.
2. Begin the game by saying, "Send me your champion who [then fill in the qualifications]."
3. The first team to send up a person who fits all the qualifications is the winner for that round. Play until a certain number of points is reached or until you just don't want to play another round.
4. The team building experience is what this activity is about. Discuss in the end how important it was to listen to all the directions before "building" your champion. Sometimes we are so eager to get going that we don't wait to get the whole picture. Then we miss some vital information, and we can't successfully complete our tasks or projects.

Ideas for Qualifications:

- Send me your champion who has on four necklaces, a ring on each finger of the right hand, one sock on the left foot and is hopping up and down on their right foot.
- Send me your champion who has on two hats, shirt sleeves rolled up, two left shoes on their feet and is holding hands with someone else on the team.
- Send me your champion who is a male, with three watches on his left arm, a pair of jeans with both pants legs rolled up and is reciting nursery rhymes.
- Send me your champion who is female, has three hats on, a toe ring, no socks but a shoe on one foot and a sandal on the other.

SENTENCE STRUCTURE

Purpose: Utilizes organizational skills, thinking-on-your-feet strategies, and cooperation. Participants in this activity work in teams to write complete sentences.

Group Size: 15 – 30 (can be done with larger groups if you make more than two teams)

Time: 10 minutes

Supplies: Newsprint and markers for each team (Check to see that the marker won't run through the paper and get on the wall or floor. It's a good idea to use washable marker.)

Directions:

1. Tape a sheet of newsprint to the wall for each team, or lay the sheets on the floor. Allow room between the sheets of paper so each team will have its own space.

2. Divide the group into equal teams and have each team line up about fifteen feet away from its paper.

3. Each team member must go to the paper, write down a word that will help form a sentence, hand off the marker to the next team member, and go to the back of the line.

4. Each person gets to write only one word. The last person to write must complete the sentence. (If there are nine people on each team, the sentence should be nine words long.)

5. No group member may talk to any other member while the sentence is being formed.

6. The first team to write a complete sentence is the winner of that round.

7. It's a good idea to give the groups a topic for each sentence, especially if you're working with a younger group.

8. Process the activity.
   - What made this difficult/easy to do?
   - Did you like the outcome of your sentence? Why?
   - How did teamwork come into play in this activity?
   - In this activity you had to think quickly about what you were going to add to the sentence. In what other areas of your life do you have to "think on your feet"?
   - Do you like to have to think/decide things quickly? Why or why not?

Variation

Have the team write a story in this same fashion. The winner can be the team with the most creative story or the team that used the most words in their story in the given amount of time.

SHOES!

Purpose: Provides an active way to get everyone relaxed and less self-conscious.

Group Size: 15 – 50

Time: 10 minutes

Supplies: None (but everyone must have a pair of shoes on)

Directions:

1. Arrange the group either in one big circle or a few small circles.
2. Have everyone take off their right shoe and toss it into the center of the circle.
3. When you say "Go," everyone should grab someone else's shoe and put it on.
4. Then have them line up by pairing up the shoes. They have to cross their right leg over someone else's left leg to make a pair.
5. End by everyone introducing themselves to their "shoemates."

SPEEDY JUGGLE

Purpose: Promotes working together to streamline a task and think beyond the obvious to solve a problem.

Group Size: 10 – 30

Time: 10 minutes

Supplies: One ball or another object to toss.

Directions:

1. Establish a pattern of tossing as described in the Group Juggle-Toss game (see page 14). Go through one cycle of tossing in that pattern.
2. Now, tell participants you are going to time them to see how fast they can do it.
3. After you establish the time for that first round, ask participants if they can think of anything they could do to speed up the toss.
4. Try one of the ideas given and time it.
5. Again, challenge them to come up with a way to do it even faster. Continue this until you've done it about as fast as you think is possible. The fastest way I've seen it done is when they figure out they can rearrange themselves so that they are next to the person they should toss to. Then they end up just passing the object from one to another around the circle. I don't give them any hints for this arrangement, though. They feel pretty good when they come up with it on their own.
6. Process this activity.
   - What can we learn from this activity?
   - How can we relate this to "real life" (our role as club member, peer helper, leader, advisor, family member)?
   - How did you feel after each attempt at cutting down the time?

THAT'S ME!

Purpose: A quick and active way to discover the make-up of your group.

Group Size: 15 - unlimited

Time: 5 minutes

Supplies: None

Directions:

1. Arrange the group in a large circle. If you have more than 100 people, have them stay in their seats.

2. Tell the group that you will call out categories, and if they fit that category, they should run to the middle of the circle, shout, "That's me!" and high-five any others who ran to the middle with them. They should do this for each category they fit into. (If you have more than 100 people and limited space, just have them raise their hands, and shout out, "That's me!")

3. Keep moving at a fast pace and have fun with this. It works well whether the participants are moving or staying in their seats.

4. Use any categories you like, but here are some ideas. Adapt them for the age group.

   - I am a senior (junior, sophomore, freshman).
   - I am from (name of state, province, city, school, or parish).
   - I am involved in a youth group.
   - I am in student council.
   - I am involved in sports.
   - I am involved in drama or music.
   - I like pizza.
   - I have a big (small) family.
   - I have a brother (sister).
   - I am an only child (middle child, oldest, youngest).
   - I was born in summer (winter, spring, fall).
   - I have a job.
   - I do volunteer work.
   - I have a pet.
   - My room is a mess (very clean).
   - I can drive.
   - I sing in a choir.
   - I have been known to sing in the shower.
   - I watch three or more hours of TV a day.
   - I read at least one book in the past month.
   - I play a musical instrument.
   - I like to eat junk food.
   - I like to eat healthy food.
   - I love to laugh.

THIS IS ME

Purpose: A low-threat activity that gives people a chance to work closely with someone for at least a minute or two. Can be done early in the formation of a group.

Group Size: 10 – 30

Time: 15 minutes

Supplies: One copy of "This Is Me" worksheet (see Appendix page 94) and a pencil for each group member.

Directions:

1. Give each participant a worksheet and a pencil.
2. Instruct everyone to mingle and find someone to pair with to draw one part of each other's face.
3. The "artists" sign their names in the spaces corresponding to the facial features they draw.
4. Then each participant should find another partner and draw one facial feature for that person, who in turn draws one of his or hers.
5. Continue this until all participants have their entire faces drawn.
6. Then have everyone sign the back of their portrait and give it to you.
7. When all are seated again, hold up each picture and have the group try to guess who it is. It's amazing how well some of the portraits turn out.

TWELVE SQUARES

Purpose: To have participants interact with and discover information about others in the group.

Group Size: 10 – 25

Time: Approximately 30 minutes (with a group of 20)

Supplies: For each participant, a "Twelve Squares" worksheet (see Appendix page 95) or a blank sheet of paper and a pen or pencil.

Directions:

1. Distribute "Twelve Squares" worksheets or have each participant fold a piece of paper into twelve squares.
2. Have each person find a partner to begin. Each is to ask the other a question that will reveal something about that person. Some typical questions are: How many people are in your family? What is the best book you ever read? Who is your favorite cartoon character? What kind of contest would you like to win?
3. Write the person's name and answer in a square. After both ask and answer one question, they move on and talk with someone else.
4. Participants may pose the same or a different question to each person. If they use a different question for each square, they should keep track of which question was asked in which square.
5. After everyone has all of their squares filled, the groups sits in a circle.
6. Ask "What did you learn about [Name]?" All who have talked with that person share their responses. The sharing should happen at a quick pace.
7. Continue until the group has heard about each member.

TWO TRUTHS AND A LIE

Purpose: Reveals some information about each participant, requires use of judgment skills, promotes discussion, and always generates laughter.

Group Size: 5 – 20

Time: 10 – 20 minutes

Supplies: 3" x 5" index card and a pen or pencil for each participant

Directions:

1. Direct participants to write their names and three facts about themselves on their index cards. Two of the facts should be true, and one should be a lie. Encourage the group to be creative.

2. In turn, have each member read his or her name and the statements on the card.

3. Other participants should vote on which statement is the lie by holding up one, two, or three fingers.

4. The votes don't really matter, but it is fun to see what everyone's guess is for the lie.

WALK THE PLANK

Purpose: Calls for strategy and cooperation—or the alligators will eat you!

Group Size: 10 – 20

Time: 20 minutes

Supplies: Masking tape or a plank-like board.

Directions:

1. If you are using tape, make a ten-foot by fourteen-inch rectangle on the floor. Adjust the length for larger groups. This is the "plank."

2. Have the group line up on the plank in order of height, shortest to tallest or vice versa. Their mission is to reverse the order of the lineup without stepping off the plank into the alligator infested waters. (You may time them to see how fast they can do this if you'd like.)

3. The leader checks that no one is stepping out of bounds. If they do, declare them "eaten by the alligators" and out of the game—or just make them go back to where they started.

4. It takes some time and teamwork to figure out the best solution to this activity. If you have more than one team, give awards for fastest time, fewest people lost to the alligators, best teamwork even without fastest time, etc.

5. Process the activity.
   - What strategy did you use to accomplish your goal?
   - Did the group change their mind many times?
   - Did anyone emerge as a leader?
   - What is the key to completing this activity successfully?
   - Where else in your life is it very important to cooperate?

THE WAVE

Purpose: Provides an activity for name introductions, following the ever-popular stadium activity—The Wave.

Group Size: 15 – 100

Time: 5 minutes

Supplies: None

Directions:

1. Arrange everyone in a circle (either sitting or standing), holding the hands of the persons on either side.
2. Have everyone find out the names of the people they are holding hands with.
3. Direct one group member, "Amy," to start the activity. Amy says the name of the person on her right, "Brian," as they raise their hands together in the air. Then Brian says the name of the person on his right, "Charlie," and they raise their hands together. Charlie says the name of the person on his right, and they raise their hands together. This pattern continues until it gets back to Amy.
4. Then reverse the flow by having Amy start the wave by speaking the name of the person on her left.
5. See how fast the group can get the wave to go around the group, first going counterclockwise, then clockwise.

WEB OF INFO

Purpose: Highlights how "connected" we can become with more information about one another.

Group Size: 10 – 20

Time: 10 – 15 minutes

Supplies: Ball of yarn or string.

Directions:

1. Have the group sit in a circle.
2. While holding a ball of yarn, ask and answer a question (see suggested questions below).
3. After answering the question, hold on to one end of the yarn and toss the ball to another participant.
4. That participant answers the question, holds onto the unwinding strand of yarn, and tosses the rest of the ball to a new person. This process continues until everyone has answered the questions and is holding onto a piece of the yarn, thus forming a spider web pattern.
5. Ask a new question and reverse the process. The one who ended up with the ball of yarn starts by answering the question and tossing the ball of yarn to the person it came from. That person rolls his or her strand of the yarn onto the ball, answers the question, and tosses it to the next person. This continues until the ball comes back to you, thus untangling the web.
6. Possible questions to ask:
   • What is your favorite time of day and why?
   • What do you think your role in this group will be?
   • What kind of store would you like to own and operate?
   • What project would you most like to carry out this year?
   • Who has influenced your life and why?
   • What is the nicest thing someone can do for another person?

WHAT'S DIFFERENT?

Purpose: Tests everyone's powers of observation, while learning to notice things about individuals.

Group Size: 6 – unlimited

Time: 5 minutes

Supplies: None

Directions:

1. Have everyone find a partner and introduce himself or herself.

2. Give the partners thirty seconds to inspect one another, taking note of things about their hair, clothing, jewelry, etc.

3. Have the partners turn back to back and quickly change something about themselves, for example, remove their earrings, switch their nametag from one side to the other, or put a pencil in their pocket.

4. Now, have the partners turn back around and see if they can spot what the other partner changed.

5. Have everyone change partners, introduce themselves, and repeat the exercise.

6. Continue the activity until time is up.

WHAT'S IN A NAME?

Purpose: Helps participants remember names and sets up a team building atmosphere.

Group Size: 10 – 50

Time: 10 minutes

Supplies: Paper and pencil for each team.

Directions:

1. Divide the group into teams of three or four people each. The teams must all have the same number of people or one team will be at a disadvantage. If this is not possible, the team(s) with fewer people should use someone's middle name for the activity.

2. Give each team a paper and pencil and have each team member write his or her first name on the top of the paper in block letters. The names can run together so that it looks like one long word. (If all but one team has four members, have the team of three use one person's first and middle names so that team will still have four names on the top of the paper.)

3. Direct the teams to make as many words as they can out of the letters at the top of their papers. Allow seven minutes for this.

4. Recognize the team with the most words as well as the team with the longest words (more than three or four letters).

ZIP, ZAP, ZOOP

Purpose: Helps people relax and have fun with a fast paced name-learning activity.

Group Size: 15 – 40

Time: 10 minutes

Supplies: None

Directions:

1. Have everyone stand in a circle. Designate one person as *It* and have *It* stand in the center of the circle.

2. Instruct *It* to point to one person in the circle, say "Zip," "Zap," or Zoop" to the person, and then count to ten out loud as fast as *It* can.

3. The person to whom *It* pointed must try to respond before *It* gets to ten.

4. If "Zip" is said, the response must be the name of the person on the responder's right.

5. If "Zap" is said, the response must be the name of the person on the responder's left.

6. If "Zoop" is said, the responder says his or her own name.

7. If *It* counts to ten before the responding person says the correct name, that person trades places with *It* and is then in the middle.

8. If the responder says the correct name, then *It* continues and points to a new person.

9. Remind players to keep things moving. It makes for a much more exciting game.

10. The game continues as long as you designate.

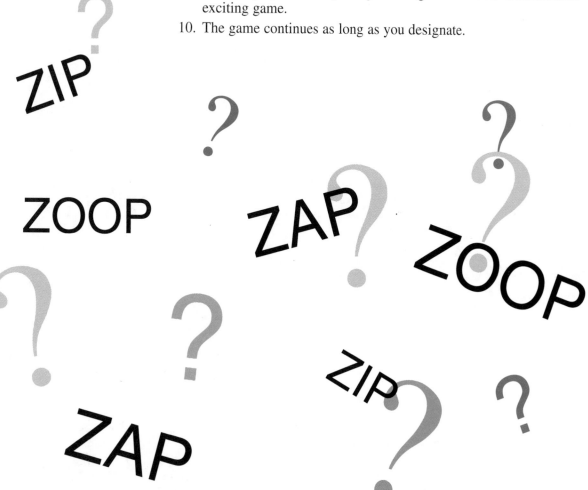

BOUNDARY BREAKING

Purpose: Provides a quiet activity in listening that can be done at any time in a group-forming process. Group members learn about one another by paying attention to tone of voice and body language.

Group Size: 10 - 30

Time: 1 - 2 hours

Supplies: Boundary Breaking Questions (see Appendix page 83).

Directions:

1. Set the atmosphere by dimming the lights in the room if possible.
2. Sit around a large table or in a circle. No one should be left out of the group, and the circle should be as tight as possible.
3. Each person should answer every question. Members may initially "pass" on a question, but you should always come back to them at a later time to answer it.
4. Read a question and invite the person to your left to answer the question first. Continue around the circle until everyone has answered. Don't forget to go back to the people who initially passed. You should be answering the questions yourself as your turn comes. There should be no debate about any answer nor should any questions be asked. It is strictly a time to listen and learn.
5. When you ask the second question, invite the second person from your left to answer first. Continue to move one person to the left for each subsequent question.
6. Try to ask as many questions as your time frame allows without rushing anyone's answer.

EAT A MEAL TOGETHER – WITH A TWIST

Purpose: Helps form a bond within the group and encourages members really to take notice of those around them.

Group Size: 6 – 15

Time: 30 – 60 minutes (maybe more if you include cleanup)

Supplies: Whatever you would need for your meal; string.

Directions:

1. Tell the group ahead of time that they are going to be eating a meal together. The meal could be pizza, spaghetti, hot dogs, or anything you like, but it should not all be on their plates when they arrive. You want them to do as much for themselves as possible to get their meal together.
2. After everyone is assembled and before you begin the meal, tie each person's wrist to the next person's wrist with a short string, so that if one person's hand moves, the person next to him or her has to move, too.
3. Things such as passing the ketchup or using a fork have to be negotiated with the person each one is next to.
4. If you'd like, have the participants clean the table and do the dishes while still connected.
5. Discuss how the group worked together and how they really had to be conscious of one another. Share funny stories about the adventure.

FIRST IMPRESSIONS

Purpose: Highlights the impact of first impressions and how different people form different impressions of the same person, incident, situation, and so forth.

Group Size: 5 – 50

Time: 15 – 20 minutes

Supplies: 4 or more pictures of people in various situations, dress, habitat; pencil and paper for each participant.

Directions:

1. Distribute paper and pencils.

2. Hold up one of the pictures and ask the participants to write down their first impression of the person in the picture. Give examples to get the group started if you think they need some ideas. For example, ask: Is this person happy...rich...nice? Does he or she have a job? Would you like to be this person's friend? What do you think this person's hobbies are? Where is this person from?

3. Hold up the next picture and have group members write "picture #2" so the impressions don't get mixed up. Again have them write their first impressions of that person.

4. Do that for a third and fourth picture.

5. Return to the first picture and ask the participants to share some of the ideas they wrote down. Do the same with the other pictures.

6. Process the activity.

   • Why did you write some of the things you did?

   • What gave you those impressions? (Do each picture separately.)

   • How do we judge one another? What characteristics do we look for?

   • Have you ever had a first impression of someone that later changed because you got to know that person? Explain.

   • What kind of impression do you think others have of you?

   • Is a first impression important?

   • How do you make a good first impression?

   • What can you do this week to change the way you judge people?

FOUR CORNERS

Purpose: Provides a simple game of grouping and re-grouping that also reveals a lot about the participants' self-assessments.

Group Size: 10 - 30

Time: 15 – 30 minutes

Supplies: None

Directions:

1. Have the group assemble in the middle of the room and remain standing.

2. Explain that you will be calling out a variety of categories and that each participant will need to decide into which category he or she belongs.

3. Explain that as you call out the categories, you will point to a specific corner of the room for each of the choices. Participants are to go to whatever corner they think "fits" them.

4. Begin by saying to the group, "Are you more like...?" and fill in the blank with one of the following options:

   - 6 a.m., noon, 6 p.m., or midnight
   - a fire truck, a pick-up truck, a school bus, or a Ferrari
   - chef salad, hamburger and fries, spaghetti, or filet mignon
   - English, social studies, art, or science
   - a golf club, a catcher's mask, swim goggles, or a bowling bag
   - a western, a comedy, a romance, or a thriller
   - a merry-go-round, swings, a slide, or monkey bars
   - Hawaii, Colorado, Washington, D.C., or Las Vegas
   - a giraffe, a tiger, a parrot, or an elephant

5. After you finish each category and all group members are in their corners, go around the room quickly and let people share a few of the reasons they chose that group. (There often is great insight and wisdom put into their choices!)

6. When that step is completed, pick another category and begin again.

7. When you are finished with categories, process the activity if you feel more discussion is helpful.

   - What did you learn about the reasons people chose their corners?
   - Were you with different people every time? Why do you think that is?
   - What were some of the most unique reasons people had for choosing a group?
   - What did you learn about others from this activity?

HOME SWEET HOME

Purpose: A self-awareness activity that provides a visual way to record and later share important information about oneself.

Group Size: 10 – 25

Time: 20 – 30 minutes

Supplies: Sheet of paper and a pencil for each participant.

Directions:

1. Have each person draw a large outline of a house. Include a door, at least two windows, a chimney, the sun, and a cloud on the sky.

2. Ask participants to think about some people and events that have influenced their lives. Give them some time to reflect before giving the following directions.

3. On the door, write the name of the person who always makes you feel at home and lets you be who you are.

4. On the bottom of the house, the foundation, write the name of the person who supports you the most.

5. On the roof, write the name of the person who helps you reach your dreams.

6. On the chimney, write something you want to tell the world.

7. On the sun, write what makes your days bright.

8. On the cloud, write one or more of your dreams.

9. When everyone is done, go around the circle and have each person share one of the things they wrote down and why. Do more if time permits.

10. If possible, hang the drawings in your group's room and let others have a chance to read them.

HOW MANY IN YOUR PARTY?

Purpose: A good mixer that helps participants learn more about their fellow group members.

Group Size: 10 – 50

Time: 15 – 30 minutes

Supplies: None

Directions:

1. Explain that you are the maitre d' at a fine restaurant and will be calling out seating arrangements for participants. You will then give them a question to discuss "at their table." Let the group mingle around the room a bit before you call out "Table for two (or three, or whatever number you choose)."

2. If you call out "table for two," group members pair off, introduce themselves, and then discuss the topic you give them. The first question could be "What are your favorite foods to eat?"

3. Give the groups a minute to discuss the question and then call out the next seating arrangement, "Table for three...six...eight, etc."

4. Each time, after the groups have formed, have them introduce themselves and discuss the question you give them.

5. Possible questions are:
   - What is something you really want to do in the next year?
   - What do you hope to get out of this workshop...class...meeting?
   - Whom can you always go to for good advice or a listening ear? Why?
   - What is your favorite thing to do outdoors?
   - What is your favorite season or holiday and why?
   - What talent would you really like to have?
   - What is/was your favorite Halloween costume?
   - When you have time to just sit and think, what do you think about?
   - Whom should you really write a letter to and why?
   - What is your favorite ride at an amusement park?

Thought Provokers

I DIDN'T KNOW THAT

Purpose: Similar to "People Bingo" (see page 19) but requires some preliminary information and preparation.

Group Size: 10 – 30

Time: 10 – 15 minutes

Supplies: "I Didn't Know That" worksheet that you will create beforehand and pen or pencil for each participant.

Directions:

1. Before this activity is used, you need to learn one funny or interesting fact about each person in the group. Make a grid worksheet incorporating these facts (see sample below) and make a copy for each person in the group.

2. At the beginning of the meeting, distribute the worksheets.

3. Tell the group members to mingle and ask one another questions to find out which fact fits which group member. When they have matched the correct person with the fact, have the person sign his or her name in the corresponding space.

4. Depending on your time and goal, you can end the activity after everyone gets a fully signed worksheet, or you can encourage discussion of the various interests.

Sample "I Didn't Know That" Worksheet

Collects comic books	Has lived in Las Vegas	Would love to have 50 cats	Likes to paint
Loves to watch old Bugs Bunny cartoons	Would love to be an actor	As a kid, wanted to be a forest ranger	Never went to Disney World
Belongs to the Medical Explorers Club	Has milked cows by hand	Owns a tarantula	Has my own web page

I GOTTA HAND IT TO YOU

Purpose: Provides a way to end a group session while focusing on something positive about each person.

Group Size: 5 – 50

Time: 15 – 30 minutes

Supplies: Paper plate or sheet of paper for each person in the group; masking tape.

Directions:

1. Give each participant a paper plate or piece of paper.
2. Direct the participants to trace one of their hands and to write their name on the plate/paper.
3. Have them make loops of masking tape, and help one another tape their paper to their backs.
4. Then have everyone circulate and take time to write on each paper or plate something they like about that person or something positive they noticed about that person. They should sign their names to what they wrote.
5. When the group is done, everyone will have an uplifting, personal keepsake to take home.

INDEX CARD THING

Purpose: Provides participants an opportunity to learn more about their fellow group members than their names.

Group Size: Unlimited

Time: 20 – 30 minutes

Supplies: An index card or sheet of paper and a pen or pencil for each participant.

Directions:

1. Have participants write answers to these six questions:
   a) What was your favorite childhood toy?
   b) What quality do you look for in a friend?
   c) What is the biggest problem in our society (school)?
   d) If you could date *anyone* in the world, whom would you date?
   e) What advice would you give your parents (principal)?
   f) What three things would you like people to say about you?
2. After the questions are answered, everyone should pair off with a partner, introduce themselves, and discuss their answers to questions a and b.
3. Next, one pair should team up with another pair, introduce themselves, and discuss questions c and d.
4. Finally, one foursome teams up with another foursome, introduces themselves, and discusses questions e and f.
5. You'll have to gauge the amount of time needed for discussion of each set of questions.

JOY / GIVE

Purpose: A good listen-and-learn activity, during which group members share things about themselves. Best done with people who know one another a bit.

Group Size: 6 – 25

Time: 20 – 30 minutes

Supplies: None

Directions:

1. Arrange group in a circle.
2. Explain that this activity is called JOY, and it will provide a chance to share some events with others in the group.
3. The letter "J" stands for *Just Did*. The first exercise, then, is to go around the circle and each person should share something he or she Just Did. (There's no time frame set for the Just Did. They can interpret that however they like.)
4. The next letter is "O" and it stands for *Ought To*. Starting with a different person, have each member tell about something he or she Ought To do.
5. The final letter is "Y," which stands for *Yourself*. Again, starting with someone new, have each person tell the group something about himself or herself.

Variation: GIVE

In place of the JOY, the letters in GIVE can be used as follows:

G - a *Goal* I recently accomplished

I- something in which I'm very *Interested*

V- a strong *Value* in me (or something/someone I really *Value*)

E- something that really affects my *Emotions*

38

MUSICAL CHAIR QUESTIONS

Purpose: Gets lots of boundary breaking questions answered in a one-on-one fashion in a short amount of time. (It usually gets pretty loud.)

Group Size: 14 – 50 people

Time: 20 minutes

Supplies: None

Directions:

1. Arrange the group into two concentric circles (an inner and outer circle) facing one another. Everyone should have a partner.

2. Ask a question and give the pairs one minute to talk about it. After the minute is up, give a direction such as "inner circle move 2 chairs to your left." The inner circle moves and the leader asks a new question. Pairs are given a minute to talk. The activity continues in that manner.

Variation

To practice listening skills, designate the inner circle as the listener and the outer circle as the talker. Give the talker one minute to answer the question while the listener practices good listening skills. Switch roles after one minute.

Some questions are suggested here, and you can use the Boundary Breaking questions on Appendix page 83.

- What are some of the best movies you've ever seen?
- What is the best thing about your hometown?
- In summer, what do you like to do?
- Whom would you like to costar with in a movie?
- What concert would you like to attend?
- What would you do with an hour of free time?
- If you could have dinner with anyone, whom would you choose?
- Describe your best friend.
- How did you feel about your last haircut?
- What is one of your pet peeves? Why?
- If you could be any cartoon character, which would you be?
- When was the last time you laughed out loud? At what?

PERSONAL CREST

Purpose: Gives everyone a chance to visually and verbally explain who they are and what they stand for.

Group Size: 5 – 25

Time: 20 minutes plus time for discussion

Supplies: A "Personal Crest" worksheet (Appendix page 90) and a pen or pencil for each participant.

Directions:

1. Give everyone a worksheet. Explain that the crest will become a symbol for the things that are important to each of them.

2. The crest is divided into seven sections with each one representing something different. Information can be recorded by either drawing or writing.

3. Give the following directions:
   - In section I, write three things you really like about yourself.
   - In section II, list the people who have influenced your life.
   - In section III, tell about an event that has been a turning point in your life.
   - In section IV, write down three things that you are thankful for.
   - In section V, write a favorite quote that guides your life.
   - In section VI, tell about what you believe in and stand for.
   - In section VII, explain your passion and purpose in life as you see it now.

4. Ask the participants to share portions of their crest entries with the group. Allow participants to ask questions of one another. This may help further clarify to the participants who they are and what they stand for.

5. The crests can be hung in the room for everyone to see or can be explained and taken home as a reminder for each person to stand for what he or she believes.

PIPE DREAMS

Purpose: An exercise for setting realistic goals and reaching them.

Group Size: 5 – 50

Time: 15 minutes

Supplies: A pipe cleaner (or chenille stem) for each person in the group.

Directions:

1. Discuss the idea of setting personal goals. Goals are dreams with deadlines. If we write down our goals, we'll have a better chance of achieving them.

2. Goals don't work unless they are "SMART" goals, an acronym for these characteristics:

   Specific

   Measurable

   Attainable

   Responsibility of the person setting the goal

   Timeline

3. Give examples.

   • If I want to be an Olympic gymnast, and I'm already thirty years old, that is not a very SMART goal.

   • If I want to *attend* the gymnastic finals at the next Olympics (specify the year), that is a SMART goal because it is realistic and attainable if I do some planning.

4. Give all participants a pipe cleaner.

5. Tell them to decide on a goal that they would like to accomplish this school year...by the end of this retreat...by next week...before this class is over. (Give them a specific time frame.)

6. Make sure they apply the SMART philosophy to it. Have them write it out if you'd like.

7. Have them form a symbol out of the pipe cleaner that will remind them of their goal.

8. Each person should share his or her goal with the group. The group can challenge the SMART aspects of the goal to help others clarify what they hope to achieve.

POSITIVE NAME EXCHANGE

Purpose: Offers an exercise for looking at the good in others and feeling good about yourself.

Group Size: 5 – 20

Time: 10 minutes

Supplies: Paper and pencil for each participant.

Directions:

1. Distribute a piece of paper and a pencil to each person in the group.
2. Each person should write his or her first name vertically down the left side of the paper.
3. Everyone passes their papers to the left. The person on the left writes something positive about the person on the right by using one of the letters in his or her name.
4. Pass the papers again and the next person writes something positive using one of the remaining letters of that person's name.
5. Keep passing the sheets of paper until all the letters in everyone's name are completed with uplifting, positive comments.
6. Return the sheets to their owners, who should keep them as a reminder of the good things that happened in the group. Or, you can have the last person to complete another's paper read that person's compliments to the rest of the group.

> **Example for the name *BRENDA*:**
>
> **B**elieves in other people
> **R**emembers my birthday
> **E**njoys helping others
> **N**ever brags about her music ability
> **D**oesn't make fun of others
> **A**lways has a smile on her face

PROMISE RINGS

Purpose: A good activity for when a group disbands—either temporarily, like at the end of a retreat, or permanently, like at graduation.

Group Size: Unlimited, but this is best done with a group of people who have been together awhile and know one another well.

Time Limit: 20 — 30 minutes, depending on group size

Supplies: For each person, an inexpensive gold or silver ring that looks like a wedding band (they can be found at party supply stores everywhere).

Directions:

1. Give everyone a ring but tell them not to put it on yet.
2. Explain that these are promise rings, and that each person is to think of something they want to promise to do or to follow through on after the group disbands (breaks camp, ends retreat, graduates, goes home). Point out that while belonging to a group, each person learns something about the others and about himself or herself. Many times, through the course of being a member of a group, a person sets a goal or gets an idea for something. It could be to meet a new person or write a letter to someone. It could be to help out at a soup kitchen or to be more patient with their siblings.
3. After everyone has thought for a few minutes, ask them to share their promise with the group. As they share their promise, tell them to put their ring on.
4. Everyone should wear their rings home as a reminder of their promise.

PUNCH BALL QUESTIONS

Purpose: An interactive, get-to-know-you activity with lightweight questions to keep the activity moving.

Group Size: 10 – 25

Time: 15 minutes

Supplies: Punch ball with questions already written on it (see Step 4).

Directions:

1. Arrange the group in a circle.
2. Tell everyone that you will start tossing the punch ball around, and when they catch it, they must answer the question that is closest to their right thumb.
3. Make sure everyone gets the punch ball once before someone gets it a second time. To help keep track of this, when the ball is being tossed, those who have not had it yet should hold their hands up. Those who have already received it should keep their hands at their sides.
4. Use your own questions or the Boundary Breaking questions on Appendix page 83. Choose the lighter-weight questions so the game moves along quickly.

SOS

Purpose: Provides an outdoor exercise in overcoming adversity through teamwork.

Group Size: 8 — 30

Time: 15 — 30 minutes

Supplies: Twigs, rocks, and branches; blindfolds.

Directions:

1. Divide the group into teams of 6 – 8 members.
2. Explain that each team is stranded on a desert island. Their goal is to build a large SOS sign on the ground so that low-flying planes will see it and rescue the group. The catch is that each team member has an impairment. One third of the members of each team is blindfolded. One third can't use their arms and must keep their hands in their pockets or at their sides. The last third of the team members cannot speak. Everyone must be included in the project for it to be a success.
3. Once the instructions are given, let each team get to work. (If there is more than one group working on this at a time, make sure they are separated a bit so they don't see how other groups are solving the problem.)
4. When the SOS is complete, process the activity:
   - How did you deal with each person's impairment and include him or her in the activity?
   - Was this easy or difficult to do? Why?
   - What did you learn from this activity that you can relate to other situations in your life?

SPIDER WEB

Purpose: Uses problem-solving skills and is designed so that all members feel comfortable taking part.

Group Size: 15 – 25

Time: 20 – 30 minutes

Supplies: Yarn or string to make the spider web; two trees about ten feet apart, if done outside; two poles if done inside.

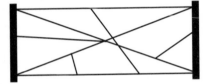

Directions:

1. The setup for this activity needs to be done ahead of time. It works really well outside with two trees about ten feet apart. Assemble the spider web by first tying the string from one tree to another at an eight foot height. Then tie another string at ground level. This is the beginning of your web.

2. Next, tie off sections to make holes big enough for people to step through or be lifted through. Count the number of people who have to get through the web and keep that in mind when deciding how many holes to make. Remember to make a couple of holes a bit more difficult than others or the group won't be challenged enough. Don't provide too many easy options. The spider web should look something like the sketch on the left when you're finished.

3. The rule is that each hole can only be used three times (four if you have a larger group). The participants have to plan and keep track of how many times a hole is used.

4. The object of this activity is to get all the players from one side of the spider web to the other by either crawling through on their own or being lifted through by others. Planning and trust are a part of this activity or it cannot be successfully accomplished.

5. Be sure to use a large gym mat under the spider web. Talk about safety before you start the activity. Someone always has to be a spotter when people are being lifted.

6. Set up the scenario with the group with some wild story like the following: "A pack of angry gazelles is after you and you must run to safety. The only way to get to the safe area is to go through the poisonous spider web. The group must get everyone through before they can go on. No one can touch any part of their body or clothing to the web or they will become motionless for one minute and cannot be passed through the web. Make your plan and get to it. Try to save everyone before the angry gazelles get to you."

7. You should step back and watch the group plan and execute their ideas. Remind them that each hole can be used only three times.

8. You can set a time limit if you want to put a little pressure on the group. Fifteen to twenty minutes is usually enough time.

9. Process the activity:
   - How did you go about planning out this activity?
   - Did everyone get a chance to share their ideas? Is that good or bad?
   - Did anyone emerge as a leader?
   - Was it easy to trust the people lifting you through the web? Why?
   - Did you run into any problems?
   - Did everyone get over safely?
   - In what other situations in real life might you have to trust someone else to make a plan or help you through a situation?

STORY LINE

Purpose: Creates a memorable experience in working together on writing a lesson with a moral.

Group Size: Unlimited—but break into groups of 3 or 4.

Time: 30 minutes

Supplies: Paper and pencil for each group.

Directions: Version 1

1. Direct each group to write a story with a moral (lesson) using all 20 key words listed below, in order. (Other words may, of course, come in between these "key" words, but as the story unfolds, the word *sun* must come first, *car* next, *laughter* next, and so on.)
2. Allow ten minutes for writing.
3. The key words to use in order are: sun, car, laughter, dark, social, two, walk, airplane, silly, blink, priceless, map, turn, pocket, run, book, pool, create, hand, fire.
4. Have each group read its story when all are finished.
5. Process this activity:
   - Why was this easy/difficult?
   - How did you decide what to write about?
   - Were you surprised by the outcome of any of the stories? Why?
   - Which story did you like the best and why?
   - Do you like working by yourself or with a group when doing activities like this? Why?
   - What are some characteristics you need to work successfully in a group?

Directions: Version 2

1. Have each group list 20 TV show titles. Give them 3 minutes to make their list. Don't tell them what they're going to do with the titles.
2. When they're finished, tell them they have to write a story with a moral using all of the titles they listed. The titles can be used in any order. Read them to the group. See if the group members can mentally note all 20 of the TV titles.
3. Process as in Version 1.

STORY TIME

Purpose: Establishes a fun atmosphere in which everyone contributes an idea. The outcome is always a surprise.

Group Size: 5 – 25

Time: 10 – 15 minutes

Supplies: Any item to toss (safely), for example, a hat, a stuffed animal, or a roll of tape.

Directions:

1. Arrange the group in a circle.
2. Ask for a volunteer to start the story.
3. The volunteer holds the object while saying the first line of a story, for instance, " It was a dark and stormy night. I was sitting on the edge of my bed when a shadow in the shape of a...."
4. Then that person tosses the object to another person, who has to pick up the story right where the last person left off. The second person adds a few lines before passing the object to someone else.
5. The goal is to keep the story going no matter how quickly the object is being tossed around.

STRENGTH BOMBARDMENT

Purpose: Gives individuals a chance to hear positive things that others have to say about them and to say positive things about others. This should be done with participants who know one another fairly well (at the end of a retreat, camp, or series of classes).

Group Size: 5 – 20

Time: 30 – 90 minutes, depending on the group size

Supplies: None

Directions:

1. Arrange group in a circle, with one member sitting in the center.
2. Each member of the circle should say a few positive words about the one in the center. Comments should be brief (10 to 20 seconds) and should be specific. (I often outlaw the words *neat, cool,* and *nice*.)
3. The person in the middle may only respond with "Thank You." He or she may not dispute what has been said. (Sometimes it is hard to accept compliments.)
4. Continue until all members have had a chance to be "bombarded" with "strengths."

If group members feel uncomfortable sitting in the middle of the circle, they may just stay on the outside of the circle.

TALKING BUDDIES

Purpose: Provides practice in good listening and sharing skills. There are no incorrect answers, only honest and dishonest ones.

Group Size: 2 – unlimited

Time: 30 minutes

Supplies: Sheet with discussion questions (see Appendix page 93) for each participant.

Directions:

1. Have everyone pair off. If there is an odd number, one group should be a group of three.
2. One person in each pair is designated the listener and the other is the speaker. (I often help this process along by saying that the one with the longest hair...the tallest...the smallest shoe size is the speaker.)
3. The speaker is to choose one of the questions and spend three minutes sharing an answer. When the three minutes are up, they should switch roles and the listener should become the speaker. Allow another three minutes for this.
4. After the first question has been answered by each person in the pair, they should choose another question and begin again.
5. If space is available, have the pairs go off to a quieter place to discuss the questions.
6. Continue the activity until the allotted time is up.

TEN NOUNS

Purpose: Helps define the concept of self-interest—discover what motivators are at work within oneself and others in the group.

Group Size: 6 – 25 works best for sharing

Time: 30 – 60 minutes

Supplies: 8 ½" x 11" sheet of paper, a pen or pencil, and a marker for each person.

Directions:

1. Give everyone a sheet of paper and pen or pencil. Ask them to write ten words that describe who they are. They are to use nouns only. It is very important that the word be a noun, not an adjective. Some examples are *female, brother, musician, Korean-American, athlete, dreamer, soprano,* and *student.*

2. Allow about five minutes to complete this first part. Then ask everyone to narrow their list to five nouns, choosing the five they feel most strongly tell who they are. They should write these on the other side of the paper with a marker. Have them write big and boldly. These can be posted in the group room to look at later if desired.

3. When everyone is finished, ask each group member to read his or her five nouns out loud in turn. If the group isn't too large or if there is plenty of time, have the members explain why they chose some of their nouns.

4. When all the sharing has taken place, discuss the following questions:

   • How many of the things listed would be visible to someone who was meeting you for the first time?

   • Were you surprised at any of the nouns?

   • What kind of questions do we need to ask if we want to get to know the real person?

   • What were some of your first impressions of the people in the group?

   • How have they changed?

   • How would knowing some of these self-interests add to the ability of the group members to get along?

UNCOMMON DENOMINATORS

Purpose: Helps group members to recognize that there are many differences among people and that those differences are valuable and necessary for working together and solving problems.

Group Size: 6 – unlimited

Time: 10 minutes, plus sharing

Supplies: None

Directions:

1. Have group members pair up and give them ten minutes to determine and discuss five things that they DO NOT have in common. They should do this by discussing attitudes, viewpoints, experiences, etc. Stress that they should look for unique or important differences—things that tell the rest of the group something about "who you are" or "who you are not." (Unacceptable comparisons are things like different color of hair or eyes, styles of homes lived in or cars driven, etc.)

2. After ten minutes, have the entire group form a circle, and have the pairs share three (or all five, if time permits) of their differences.

3. Process the activity with the following questions:
   - What did you learn about the members of the group?
   - Why is it useful to understand differences?
   - When solving problems in your church, school or community, why might it be valuable to have differences?
   - What would be important to keep in mind in a group setting, knowing that there are many different viewpoints or experiences?
   - If you were forming a committee, would you invite someone with a differing view to join that committee? Why or why not?

UNIQUELY ME!

Purpose: To think about and then share traits about oneself.

Group Size: Unlimited

Time: 30 — 45 minutes

Supplies: Sheet of paper and a pen or pencil for each participant.

Directions:

1. Have each participant trace one of their hands on a piece of paper.

2. In each finger (and thumb) list the following:
   - something I'm proud of
   - two of my good friends
   - something I like about myself
   - a person I want to be like and why
   - what I most vividly see in my future

3. On the palm of the hand, have everyone write two things they enjoy doing.

4. After everyone has finished writing, ask each person to share at least one response.

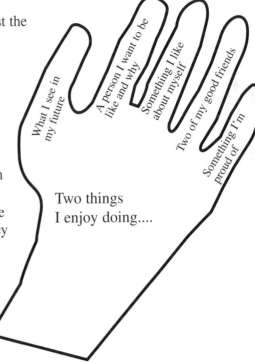

What I see in my future

A person I want to be like and why

Something I like about myself

Two of my good friends

Something I'm proud of

Two things I enjoy doing....

WHAT I LIKE ABOUT ME IS...

Purpose: Encourages group members to talk about themselves, and gives each member a chance to share things that may not come out in a large group discussion.

Group Size: 10 – 20

Time: 5 – 10 minutes

Supplies: None

Directions:

1. Have members pair up. One person of the pair is "A" and the other is "B."

2. Have the B's begin. For one minute, B should tell A, "What I like about me is...." Every sentence must begin with "What I like about me is..." and there is no pausing allowed. (Example: What I like about me is that I help out when I am asked. What I like about me is that I like nature. What I like about me is that I like to laugh. What I like about me is that I'm nice to my brother.)

3. After all the B's and A's have finished, discuss with everyone about how it feels to talk about yourself. (Especially for a whole minute!)

4. Also, discuss what each group member learned about the other person.

YES/NO LINE

Purpose: Looks at the values of group members and lets each person take a stand on a question/situation.

Group Size: 5 – 30

Time: 30 minutes

Supplies: None

Directions:

1. Explain that you will present some situations, and each person will be given a chance to agree, disagree, or stand somewhere in the middle on the issue. One side of the room will be the Yes/Agree side and the opposite side will be the No/Disagree side. Group members can stand anywhere along that imaginary line to indicate their positions.

2. Once members have taken a "stand," ask some of them why they chose that position on the line, and allow discussion on the issue.

3. The level of the statement/question should be appropriate to how well the group knows one another. These are some ideas for starters:

   - It's OK to cheat on a test.
   - If I found a wallet with $50 in it and no identification, I would keep the money.
   - I owe my parents my best effort in all I do because they raised me.
   - A little white lie never hurts anyone.
   - I would tell my best friend if I saw his or her boyfriend or girlfriend cheating on him or her.
   - The best way to get ahead in life is to go to college and get an education.
   - If something is bugging me about my friend, it's always best to tell him or her.
   - My faith in God can get me through anything.
   - You've been working hard in class all year and a classmate wants to copy your notes. This person rarely pays attention in class. Do you let the person copy?
   - As a famous athlete, you are offered $200,000 to endorse a product you would never use. Do you endorse the product?
   - At lunch, your friends are criticizing one of your friends who isn't there. Do you speak up for this friend?
   - You get two really good seats on the bus hoping the attractive person you see will sit next to you. An old man asks for the seat first. Do you give it to him?
   - You've accepted a date when someone you'd much rather go out with calls and asks you out for the same night. Do you try to get out of the first date?
   - You told your parents you were on your way to church. On your way there, a friend sees you and asks you to come to the mall instead. Do you go to the mall?

Thought Provokers

ALPHABET DANCING

Purpose: Good exercise in healthy competition, instant cooperation, and organization. Works well in helping a group of strangers get to know one another. (One of my personal favorites.)

Group Size: 20 – 40

Time: 10 minutes

Supplies: Two sets of index cards with capital letters of the alphabet written on each (one letter per card for a total of 52 cards)

Directions:

1. Divide the group into two teams.
2. Arrange a set of alphabet cards on each of two chairs or tables that are set fifteen to twenty feet away from two starting lines.
3. Direct each team to stand behind one of the starting lines.
4. Have your list of words ready (see suggestions below) and when you call out a word, each team must send a player for each letter of the word to the stack of cards. They must find the correct letters and hold them up in the proper order so that you can read the word. For, instance, if you say CAT, three people run to the letters, grab one C, one A, and one T. Then they must arrange themselves in order, and hold up the cards so that you can read the word CAT.
5. The team who spells the word correctly first gets a point. After the word is spelled, the letters should be returned to the stack. You can play until one team has earned a designated number of points or until you've exhausted your list of words. Whoever has the most points at that time wins.
6. Sometimes it's good to have two referees watching the competition, and they can rule on who completed the spelling first.
7. Suggested words to use:

dreams	outlaw	New York	harmonic
goals	listen	angels	symbolic
driveway	quietly	thunder	rhyme
chemistry	laughter	wishful	holiday

8. With just the 26 letters of the alphabet, you are limited to words with no duplicate letters. If you want to add another E, T, S, R, A or L to the set of letters, you can spell many more words.

BALLOON TRAIN

Purpose: A team activity that requires a lot of cooperation among members.

Group Size: Teams of 8 to 10

Time: 10 minutes

Supplies: large balloon for each person; one chair or cone for each team

Directions:

1. Have each team of 8 – 10 form a single line behind the starting point. Have a chair or cone about thirty feet away to serve as the turn-around point.
2. Ask each person, except the head of the line, to blow up a balloon.
3. One balloon goes between each person on the team, so the members must be close enough to one another to keep the balloons from falling to the ground.
4. The object of the game is to see which team can go from the starting point, around the chair or cone, and back to the starting point the fastest without losing any balloons.

Variation:

Make the course more of an obstacle course by arranging things in the way of the team members: they may have to go over chairs, under branches, around objects, or through narrow spaces.

BIRD ON A PERCH

Purpose: Provides a fast-action competition that is a lot of fun.

Group Size: 20 – 100

Time: 15 minutes

Supplies: Music (radio or tape/CD player).

Directions:

1. Have each player get a partner.
2. Form an inner and outer circle with one partner in the inner circle and one partner in the outer circle. The partners should stand facing each other.
3. When the music starts, the inner circle moves clockwise and the outer circle moves counter-clockwise. When the music stops, the partners must run to each other. One partner gets down on one knee and the other partner sits on that knee. Then they must freeze.
4. The last set of partners to get down on one knee is out of the game. Any other pair that moves—doesn't stay frozen—until the music starts again, is also out of the game.
5. Play until only one pair is left.

BLINDFOLD BOWLING

Purpose: To learn teamwork and communication.

Group Size: 10 – 20

Time: 15 – 30 minutes

Supplies: Plastic bowling balls and pins; blindfolds.

Directions:

1. Divide the group into two teams.
2. Set up the pins as you would in a normal bowling game, about 25 – 30 feet away from the bowler.
3. Blindfold the first bowler and spin him or her around seven times.
4. The people on that bowler's team can give directions so the bowler will be in the vicinity of the pins but they cannot touch the bowler. The bowler must throw the bowling ball before fifteen seconds elapse.
5. Keep a record of the number of pins knocked down after each player tosses the bowling ball one time.
6. Alternate bowlers between the two teams. The winning team is the one with the highest score.
7. Discuss how each team communicated with its blindfolded bowlers and how that helped or hindered their bowling ability.

BOP 'EM

Purpose: Gets everyone involved. Particularly good energizer between long listening sessions.

Group Size: Unlimited groups of 5 - 7 people

Time: 5 minutes

Supplies: 2 balloons for each group.

Directions:

1. Divide any large group into smaller groups of 5 to 7 people.
2. Blow up one balloon for each group. (The second can be used as a reserve if the first one pops, or you can add it to the game if you want to make it more difficult.)
3. Each group holds hands and sees how long they can keep the balloon in the air by only using their head and elbows to keep it up. Have them count the number of times it is hit legally.
4. Next, have the group only use their feet and knees. Again, have them count the number of times it stays in the air legally.
5. Then have them try their knees and their hands that are still clasped together. The point of this game is to work together and have fun.

COUNT OFF

Purpose: Can be a problem-solving activity but is mostly used as an energizer and to get the group working together. It's fun and harder than you might think!

Group Size: 10 – 40

Time: 5 – 10 minutes

Supplies: None

Directions:

1. Participants may be standing in no particular order, or they may be sitting at desks or on the floor.

2. Tell the group to count from one to ten. Sounds easy, but these are the guidelines.

    a) Only one person may say a number at a time.

    b) No one person may say two or more consecutive numbers.

    c) The numbers must be said in sequence.

    d) If more than one person says a number at the same time, the group must start over.

    e) No other talking may occur once the counting begins.

3. When you say "Go," the counting begins.

4. If the group is really having trouble, stop the game, and tell them they can make up one rule. It's interesting to see how that can speed the game along.

5. Process the activity with the following questions:

- Was this a tough task? Why or why not?
- How did you establish a pattern?
- What verbal and non-verbal clues did you use to know who would go next?
- What would make your task easier?
- How can you relate this to habits of communication?

DECK OF CARDS - LABELING

Purpose: Demonstrates how we label one another before really getting to know one another.

Group Size: 15 – 50

Time: 10 minutes

Supplies: Deck of cards.

Directions:

1. Give everyone in the group a card and tell them NOT to look at it yet.
2. After everyone has a card, tell them to hold their card on their forehead so that the other group members can see it.
3. Everyone should then mingle around the room and react to people according to the following standards:
   - People with Aces, Kings, Queens, or Jacks should be treated with the most respect. These are the people to know. Seek them out.
   - Those with twos, threes, or fours should be avoided at all costs.
   - Those whose cards are numbered from five through ten should be treated at an appropriate level according to their number, that is, they should be spoken to but not in depth or for very long.
4. Let the group mingle for about two minutes, and then have everyone guess what card they have. After that, they can look at their cards.
5. Process the activity with these or other questions of your own:
   - What card did you think you had on your forehead?
   - In what ways did the others in the group react to you?
   - How did those with low cards feel during this activity?
   - How did those with high cards feel during this activity?
   - What kind of things do we notice when we label people?
6. After processing the activity, stress that we need to treat one another as the "high cards" if we truly want to make a difference.

ELECTRICITY

Purpose: Gets everyone involved in a fun exercise of teamwork and competition.

Group Size: 15 – 40 people

Time: 10 – 30 minutes

Supplies: Coin; object to grab at end of line.

Directions:

1. Before you start the competition, decide on a stopping point. You can set a score limit (five points is usually enough) or stop the game after each person has had a chance to be a line leader.

2. Form the group into two even lines, with each person in line facing a member of the other team. Decide which end of the line is the head. The person at the head of the line is the line leader.

3. Place an object to be picked up at the end of the line, equidistant from the last persons in the two lines (they will be the "grabbers"). There should be only one object for the two lines. Some objects you might use are a stuffed animal, a roll of tape, or a ball of yarn.

4. Instruct all teammates to hold hands and all except the line leaders should close their eyes.

5. The leaders should keep their eyes on you as you flip a coin. Hold the coin up to allow the leaders to see whether it landed on heads or tails.

6. If it is heads, each line leader squeezes the hand he or she is holding, and the squeeze should get passed down the line as quickly as possible. When the last person feels the squeeze, he or she should grab the object at the end and hold it up. That team is awarded one point!

7. If it is tails, no squeeze should be started. If one of the line leaders mistakingly starts the squeeze and it reaches the end of the line, that team loses one point. If no one squeezes, you'll know after a few seconds by the lack of reaction. Then go on to the next toss.

8. Once the line leaders have had a chance to squeeze hands (after the first toss that lands heads), they go to the end of the line and the next two people become the line leaders. The game continues in the same way.

FIVE FAST FILL-INS

Use as quick lessons, energizers, or for short breaks. Most can be done with a group of any size. Paper and pen or pencil needed in some cases.

Attitude

Have everyone write out the word *ATTITUDE* on a piece of paper. Assign a number value to each letter of the word: A=1, B=2, C=3, D=4, and so on. Once they get the letter values assigned, have them add the totals for the word *ATTITUDE*. It should add up to 100. Discuss how everything you do in life comes down to your attitude about it. Having a positive attitude will help you get 100% out of life.

N or M States?

Ask the group to get in groups of two or three quickly. Tell them they have one minute to figure out the answer to this question: "Are there more states that start with the letter *M* or the letter *N*?" After one minute ask for a show of hands from those who think there are more states with the letter *M*?" Then do the same for the letter *N*. They will be surprised to learn that there are eight states that begin with each of these letters. See if they can think of all sixteen states.

20 Words in 20 Seconds

Have the group get in groups of three. Tell them to think of twenty words in twenty seconds that do not have the letter A in them. It's fun to see what they come up with in that short amount of time. It seems that when you mention the letter A, you can't help but focus on the letter A and this simple exercise becomes difficult. (Quick Solution: Count from one to twenty. You've just listed twenty words without the letter A in them. In fact, all the numbers up to one thousand do not have the letter A in them.)

Hand Clasp - Habits

Tell everyone to stretch their arms out in front of them. Then have them clasp their hands together, fingers interlocking. Tell them to look at which thumb is on the top. Is it the left or right? Now have them change their grip so that the opposite thumb is on the top. Usually, it feels very strange and unfamiliar. The lesson here is that change is often very uncomfortable. But if you clasped your hands the opposite (uncomfortable) way for twenty-one days, it would start to feel "normal" because new habits take that long to get established. Point out how helpful this can be when trying to acquire good habits. Variation: Do the same exercise with crossing your arms. It's harder and funnier to watch.

What Color Is This?

Hold up a white piece of paper and ask the group, "What color is this?" They will answer, "White." Ask again, "What color is this?" They again should say, "White." Ask two more times, each time getting the answer "white." Finally ask, "What do cows drink?" Most of the group will say "milk." They'll know you got them because they will realize quickly that the answer should have been "water." Use this just for fun or to talk about how easily we can get thrown off the right track by diversions. Variation: Ask a group this series of questions.

1. What do bunnies do to move? (Hop)
2. What is on a long stick and used for cleaning?(Mop)
3. What is another word for Dad? (Pop)
4. The opposite of bottom is ___. (Top)
5. What do you do at a green light? (Go) Most will answer Stop.

GETTING INTO GROUPS

Energizers

Purpose:
Provides creative options for dividing into groups.

Pairing Up

- Everyone hold up either a thumb or a pinky. All the thumbs should find one another and all the pinkies should find one another.
- Everyone stand on one foot. Find a partner who is on the opposite foot.
- Everyone secretly pick a vacation spot (give two choices, like the Bahamas or Colorado; Disney World or Sea World). Pair up with someone who is going to the same place.
- Pair up with the first person you meet who is wearing one of the same colors as you.
- Make the sound of a cat or a dog. Pair up with the first person you hear making the same sound.
- Call out "Chocolate" or "Vanilla." Pair up with someone who chose the same flavor as you.

Using a Deck of Cards (Give a card to everyone.)

- Get together with the same numbers of all the suits (groups of four).
- Get together with the same suit (groups of 13 or less). Note: You control the number of each suit in the deck according to how many groups you want.
- Find the best poker hand (group of five).
- Find a pair (group of two).
- Get one of each suit in your group (group of four).

Animal Noises

As people arrive, give them a slip with an animal's name on it, or whisper it in their ear. Use as many different animals as you need teams. Tell everyone to close their eyes, make the animal sound, and try to find the others in their group just by following the sounds.

Nametags

Put a colored dot or identifying sticker on each nametag before the gathering starts. (If you need five groups, use five distinctive dots or stickers.) When you are ready to break into groups, tell everyone to check their nametag and find the others who belong to their group.

Phone Number

Tell the group to pretend that the meeting room is the keypad of a touch tone phone. They need to think of the last digit of their home phone numbers and go to the space in the room that would correspond to that number on the keypad. (You most likely will end up with uneven group sizes.)

GETTING INTO GROUPS (cont'd)

Humdingers

Determine how many teams you need. Give each player a strip of paper that has a childhood song on it. Or you can whisper the name of the song in their ear. Some examples are: "Happy Birthday," "Mary Had a Little Lamb," "Row, Row, Row Your Boat," "Twinkle, Twinkle, Little Star." Everyone hums their song and forms a group with any person humming the same song.

Puzzlers

Cut pictures out of magazines. Make sure each picture is distinctly different from the others. Cut each picture into as many pieces as you need members in each group. Mix up all the pieces and have people draw a piece out of a bag. The challenge is to find others with pieces from the same picture. When they find each other, they put the picture back together.

Clipped Together

Decide how many groups you need and use that same number of different colors of paper clips. Mix all the clips together and have everyone pick one and find all the others with that same color. They should then make a long paper clip chain with their group members.

Seasons

Have everyone count off by saying *spring, summer, fall,* or *winter.* To form four groups, everyone from each season should get together. To form a group of four people, one from each season should get together.

Whatevers

Determine how many teams you want. That is the number of categories you need. For instance, if you need two teams, have everyone find a partner and decide between them who wants to be an apple and who wants to be an orange (or a sun/moon; refrigerator/freezer; 100/200). Once they've decided, tell all the apples to get on one side and all the oranges to go to the other side. If you want three teams, you could use sun/moon/stars or Huey/Dewey/Louie. For four teams, you could use spring/summer/fall/winter, and so on.

GIANT EGG DROP

Purpose: Highlights creativity in team work.

Group Size: 10 – 50

Time: 20 – 30 minutes

Supplies: Fill a paper lunch bag with the following items for each team: 2 tongue depressors, 4 rubber bands, paper cup, 1 sheet of newspaper, 10 toothpicks, 1 foot of masking tape, 1 raw egg.

Directions:

1. Divide the group into teams of four or five.
2. Give each group a bag of supplies.
3. Tell them they have fifteen minutes to construct something that will help their egg survive a two-story drop.
4. After time is up, allow each group to show off their design.
5. Discuss which design everyone thinks will work the best.
6. Test each design by dropping it out of a two-story building or from a fifteen-foot height onto a hard surface.
7. Process the activity.

   - Whose design worked the best? Was it the same one you predicted?
   - How did you feel about your group's design after it was completed?
   - How did you go about designing your egg protector? Were ideas from all team members used or was one person's idea used?
   - Did you give all of your input or did you hold back some of your ideas from the group? When have you done that at other times in your life?
   - Did you believe your groups idea would work? Why or why not?
   - What did you learn from this activity?

HANDS DOWN

Purpose: Gets a group to work together and solve a problem.

Group Size: Unlimited

Time: 10 minutes

Supplies: None

Directions:

1. Arrange groups of four.
2. Instruct groups that they must devise a way to support themselves one inch off the floor or ground for five seconds on their hands only. Group members must be touching one another "so that a current of electricity could pass through your group." Only hands may touch the ground. Other objects, such as chairs, walls, desks, and so on, may not be used.

Solutions

Many creative solutions can be found. Two of the most common are:

- The group forms a square with each person face down and in a push-up position. Each person's feet are on another's person's back. On the count of three, everyone "lifts," creating one big square push-up.
- The group forms a square, having each person sitting facing the side of another person in the square. Each person's legs are straight out with the feet resting on the next person's thighs. Everyone puts their hands behind them, and on the count of three, the whole group lifts up at once. "Leverage" is the key to this activity.

HOW MANY SQUARES?

Purpose: Shows how working together can help achieve greater success and more accuracy.

Group Size: Unlimited

Time: 10 minutes

Supplies: Copy of the squares diagram (see Appendix page 86) and a pen or pencil for each participant.

Directions:

1. Distribute the diagrams and have each person count the squares and write his or her answer on the page.
2. Break up the groups into threesomes and have each group reach a consensus on how many squares they can find. (You should find 40 squares at least. Very creative people find even more!)
3. Process the activity with the group.
   - How many squares did you count on your own?
   - How many squares did you count with your group?
   - Which count was more accurate? Why?
   - What advantages/disadvantages are there to working in a group?
   - In what way do you work best—in a group or alone? Why is that a good thing to know about yourself and to know about other people you may have to work with?

Solution:

1	2	3	4
5	6	7	8
9	10	11	12
13	14	15	16

17: 17a 17b 17c 17d

18: 18a 18b 18c 18d

Quantity of Squares	Sizes and Combinations
1	square made up of squares 1 through 16
18	squares (1 through 18)
9	squares from the following combinations:

1+2+5+6   6+7+10+11
2+3+6+7   7+8+11+12
3+4+7+8   9+10+13+14
5+6+9+10   10+11+14+15
　　　　　　11+12+15+16

8	squares identified as the following:

17a   18a
17b   18b
17c   18c
17d   18d

4	squares from the following combinations:

1+2+3+5+6+7+9+10+11
2+3+4+6+7+8+10+11+12
5+6+7+9+10+11+13+14+15
6+7+8+10+11+12+14+15+16

40

HUMAN BRIDGE

Purpose: Promotes teamwork, trust, and creative
thinking.

Group Size: Unlimited

Time: 10 minutes

Supplies: Two chairs per
group.

Directions:

1. Arrange participants in groups of 8 – 10 people.
2. Explain that each group must form a bridge from one chair to the other,
"so the lightweight troll from another village can walk over them to the
other side of the cliff and get the power food needed to survive in the
wilderness," but...

   only four *hands* can be touching the ground

   only three *feet* can be touching the ground

   only two *derrieres* can be touching the ground

   only two *people* can be touching the chairs

3. Let the group go for five minutes. If it's too easy, reduce the number of
feet or hands allowed. If it is absolutely too hard, allow another five
minutes and let them use another foot. You'll have to use your own
judgment to make the challenge fit your group.
4. After the bridge is completed, ask the participants to comment on the
activity.
   - Who took the role as the leader and who were the followers?
   - Did anyone feel like his or her ideas were left out?
   - In what ways is being a team important?
   - How can building a human bridge relate to real life?

I CAN FIND THAT!

Purpose: Promotes teamwork
and provides challenges
that are harder than they
appear to be.

Group Size: 6 – 50 or more,
depending on the size of
the room. I've done it with
up to 100.

Time: 10 – 20 minutes

Supplies: Objects to hide
around the room; item
sheet for each participant
(see Appendix page 87 or
make your own).

Directions:

1. Hide small objects around the room before anyone arrives at the gathering. Be creative about hiding things but make sure they remain in plain
view so that nothing has to be disturbed.
2. Divide the large group into smaller groups of two to four (see "Getting
into Groups," page 58)
3. Give each participant an item sheet and tell them to find as many items
on the list as possible before the time expires. Group members must
stay together while searching for the objects. All objects found must be
recorded on the sheet in order to get credit. No items are to be moved
once they are spotted. Warn the participants that they should try to not
let on to other teams when or where they spot an item.
4. The team who finds the most items within the allotted time wins.
5. You can set the amount of time, but ten minutes is a good starting point.

ICEBERGS AHEAD

Purpose: A good lesson in creative problem solving.

Group Size: 15 – 25

Time: 15 – 30 minutes

Supplies: Tarp or blanket.

Directions:

1. Explain that the group must get everyone aboard the ship (blanket/tarp) because the water is icy cold and everyone must survive the ocean voyage.

2. Lay the blanket on the ground and have everyone get aboard. Set a time limit for getting everyone on the boat. The blanket should be of a size that would allow the whole group to fit without too great of a challenge. They are allowed to get on top of one another.

3. Tell the group they must all stay aboard for ten seconds. (That's about the time it takes to sing "Row, Row, Row Your Boat.")

4. Next, inform the group that their boat just hit an iceberg, and they were all thrown off the boat. (They must get off the blanket now.)

5. Fold the blanket a little smaller and tell the group to reboard what's left of the boat. It should be a bit more difficult this time. They must stay on the boat for another ten seconds.

6. Again, the boat hits an iceberg. Everyone must get off the boat. Fold the blanket a little smaller and have the group try one more time to get everyone aboard the remaining planks for ten seconds. Make this last time very difficult by folding the blanket quite small.

7. Tip: It helps to have a couple of spotters, especially for the last round.

8. Process the activity.
   - What was the initial goal? How did it change?
   - What made the activity easy/difficult to do?
   - What actions do you take when you're dealt with setbacks?
   - Do you adjust easily to change? Why?
   - What feelings did you have during this activity? Can you relate those feelings to events that happen in everyday life?
   - What did you notice about yourself during this activity?

JUST LIKE CLOCKWORK

Purpose:
Demonstrates how cooperation is necessary to achieve a common goal.

Group Size: 20 – 100

Time: 15 minutes

Supplies: A stop watch or any watch or clock with a sweep hand.

Directions:

1. Have everyone hold hands in a large circle.

2. Choose a person to be the starting point and either put a marker there or stand there yourself.

3. Tell the group to move clockwise 360 degrees. When the starter person reaches the marker, the whole group should change direction and go 360 degrees counterclockwise. They are virtually running in a circle one way and then back the other.

4. Time the group to see how long it took them to complete the activity, one movement clockwise and one movement counterclockwise.

5. Then have them try it again to see if they can beat their record.

6. Continue trying to beat each previous record for as long as your time allows.

KNOTS

Purpose: Gets a group feeling relaxed and close.

Group Size: Unlimited, but a very large group will have to break into smaller groups of 6 – 10.

Time: 15 minutes

Supplies: None

Directions:

1. Have all group members raise their hands in the air and grab the hands of other people in their group, keeping these restrictions in mind:
   - Each hand must connect to a different person.
   - No one can hold hands with the person on either side of them.
2. After everyone is connected, tell them to untangle without letting go of hands.
3. The prize is the satisfaction of working together and solving the problem.

LINE UP

Purpose: Shows that we can communicate in ways other than verbal.

Group Size: 15 – 50

Time: 10 minutes

Supplies: None

Directions:

1. Tell the group to line up by birthday month and day (not year), so that January is on one side of the room and December is on the other. They *cannot* talk to one another while doing this.
2. Don't give them too many other directions. They figure out quickly how to work together and get the line correct.
3. When they seem to be all done, have each person say his or her birthday month and day. Continue down the line to see if everyone is in order.
4. Process the activity.
   - Was this difficult for the group? Why or why not?
   - How did you communicate when you were told you couldn't talk?
   - Did a leader emerge from the group? Was that helpful? Why?
   - What would make this easier to do?

Variation

Line up by last names, shoe sizes, heights, or grades.

LOGIC PUZZLERS

Directions:

1. Explain that you will give the group a puzzle to solve. You will only answer yes or no questions.
2. Structure the activity so that either questions can be asked at random or that each person must have asked one question before someone asks a second question.
3. Anyone can guess the answer at any point in the activity. There is no penalty for a wrong answer.

PUZZLERS

a. A man comes home from work each day to his high-rise apartment. He gets into the elevator, proceeds to the ninth floor, leaves the elevator, and walks up to his apartment on the fifteenth floor. In the morning, he gets on the elevator on the fifteenth floor, goes to the ground floor, and goes to work. This happens each day unless it's raining. Why?

b. Mary and John are found in a locked hotel room. Windows are also locked from the inside. Mary is lying dead on the floor. Around Mary there is a stain and pieces of glass. John is sound asleep on the bed. What happened?

c. A man was afraid to go home because of the man in the mask. Who was the man in the mask?

d. A woman goes into a bar and asks for a glass of water. The bartender reaches under the bar and points a gun at her. Why?

e. A man was writing a letter. All of a sudden there was a power failure and he died. Why?

f. Dave, Sam, and Mary were discovered in a room by the police. Mary was dead. Dave was holding a smoking gun. The police arrested Dave and the judge convicted him, yet he was given his freedom. Why?

g. A man was found dead, lying in a meadow. He had a ring in his hand and he had on a backpack. How did he die?

h. There are two rooms, side by side. There is a door through which you can go from one room to the other. The door is shut and you are allowed to go through it only one time. In the first room, there are three light switches. In the second room, there are three light bulbs. How can you tell which light switch controls which bulb?

(See answers on next page.)

LOGIC PUZZLERS (cont'd)

ANSWERS

a. The man is a midget. The elevator is self operated, and he couldn't reach any higher. If it was raining, however, he could use his umbrella to reach the buttons.

b. Mary was a fish in a bowl. John accidentally knocked the bowl off the bed in his sleep.

c. This man is a baseball player running to home plate. The man in the mask is the catcher.

d. The woman asking for water had the hiccups and the bartender pointed the gun at her to scare her out of the hiccups.

e. The man was a skywriter. The power failure caused his plane to crash.

f. Dave and Sam were Siamese Twins.

g. The ring is from a parachute. The backpack is a parachute.

h. Turn on one switch and leave it on for a few minutes. Then turn it off and turn a second switch on. Go through the door. The bulb that is lit is the one controlled by the second switch. Feel the other two bulbs. The one that is warm to the touch was the one turned on by the first switch. The remaining bulb is controlled by the last switch.

A LOTTA HOT AIR

Purpose: Promotes team work while having a lot of fun.

Group Size: 16 — unlimited

Time: 10 — 15 minutes

Supplies: One straw per person; two facial tissues for each team.

Directions:

1. Divide the group into two equal teams. (If you have a very large number of participants, break into teams of eight to ten players.)
2. Have each team form a line.
3. Give each participant a straw.
4. Explain that when you say "Go," the first person in line is to suck the tissue into the end of the straw and then pass it to the next person in line. That person must suck the tissue into his or her straw and pass it to the next person in line. The tissue does not have to be completely inside the straw, just enough that it should not fall out.
5. No hands may be used. If the tissue falls to the floor, the team member who last had the tissue must suck it off the floor with his or her straw.
6. The team that gets a tissue to the end of the line first is the winner.

LUCKY THIRTEENS

Purpose: Stresses basic addition skills when used with younger children and cooperation and teamwork with any age group.

Group Size: 10 — 50

Time: 5 — 10 minutes

Supplies: None

Directions:

1. Divide group into teams of four or five.
2. Have the members of each group face one another and hold one fist out in front of them.
3. On the count of three, each group member holds up from zero to five fingers. The object is to have the total fingers held up within the group equal thirteen. Naturally, no one may talk or plan how to do this before the game starts. It probably will take a few tries to get the lucky thirteen.
4. Change the lucky number for another round.

MONSTER WALK

Purpose: Promotes team-work, cooperation and creativity.
Group Size: Unlimited
Time: 10 minutes
Supplies: None

Directions:

1. Divide the group into teams of five to ten people.
2. Explain that each group must join themselves together to form a single monster that walks with hands and feet on the ground. The monster must have one more foot than the number of people in the group and one less hand than the number of people in the group. For instance, if there are five people in the group, there must be six feet and four hands on the ground.
3. Once the monster is created, it must move five feet in any direction and make a sound.
4. Allow five to ten minutes for the groups to decide how to create their monsters.
5. Have each group go to the front of the room and do their monster walk.

MOOSE, COUCH POTATO, MOSQUITO

Purpose: Provides a quick energizer.
Group Size: Unlimited
Time: 5 minutes
Supplies: None

Directions:

1. Have everyone pair off and stand with backs facing each other.
2. Explain that each person must decide, silently, if he or she is going to be a moose, couch potato or mosquito.
3. On the count of three, the partners should both turn around quickly and make the appropriate faces and arm motions (see below).
4. The game continues until both partners match when they turn around.
5. For an extra challenge, try it in groups of threes.

Faces and Motions

Moose: Hold up both hands on either side of head (like antlers).

Couch Potato: Fold hands together on one side of head (like you're sleeping).

Mosquito: Pull down the skin under the eyes with pointer and middle finger of one hand; use other pointer finger to make a stinger alongside your nose.

MURDER / WINK

Purpose: Provides a low-threat interaction game.

Group Size: 15 – 50

Time: 15 minutes

Supplies: None

Directions:

1. Tell all players to close their eyes and hold out their thumbs behind their backs.
2. Explain that you will squeeze one of the extended thumbs to indicate that that person will be the murderer.
3. When you say "okay," the players should open their eyes and walk around the room, shaking hands and smiling at others.
4. When someone is winked at, he or she must count silently to five, then loudly and dramatically die by falling to the floor.
5. If a player thinks he or she knows who the murderer is, he or she can say, "I'd like to make an accusation. I think the murderer is_____."
6. If the player is right, that player becomes the leader. If the player is wrong, he or she must die a dramatic death and fall to the floor.
7. The game then continues as before until someone makes a correct accusation. It seldom gets all the way down to two people before someone makes the correct accusation.

NAME THAT TUNE

Purpose: Gets everyone involved through a challenging activity that uses a favorite medium—music.

Group Size: Unlimited

Time: 15 minutes

Supplies: Audiotape with 20 - 35 song snippets that you've pre-recorded (see Note); one sheet of paper and a pen or pencil for each group; cassette player.

Directions:

1. Divide a large group into groups of four to six people.
2. Tell them you are going to play a tape of song clips and they are to write down the title and artist of each clip. You will play the tape from beginning to end one time only. The tape will not be played a second time.
3. Give one point for each correct song and one point for each correct artist.
4. When the tape is done, read the correct answers. The group with the highest score wins.

Note: It is best to include all types of music—classical, rock, country, Christmas, jazz, blues, soundtracks—and from different eras. The library is a good resource for music that you may not have at home. Make a list of the song titles and artists in the order you recorded them. That will be your answer key. Don't allow a large gap of silence between songs. Keep it moving along.

NEWSPAPER FASHION SHOW

Purpose: Use organizational skills to accomplish a specific task.

Group Size: 30 – 50, in groups of 6 – 10 people each

Time: 30 – 40 minutes

Supplies: A stack of newspapers per group (about the size of an average metropolitan Sunday edition); partial roll of masking tape per group.

Directions:

1. Tell each group to organize a fashion show, using only newspaper, tape, and their creativity.

2. Explain that each group must develop a theme for their show. (Examples: World of Weddings, Cartoon Capers, Costumes from Outer Space, The 1500s.)

3. The groups must decide who will be their fashion designers and who will be their models.

4. They also need to decide who will emcee their show and who will write the exciting and detailed commentary.

5. Allow about twenty minutes for the planning and designing stage. At the end of this time, assemble everyone together and have each group present their show.

6. Time should be left at the end for processing the activity.

   - How did you come up with your ideas?
   - What organizational skills were used?
   - How was it decided who would do what? Are some people better suited to certain tasks? Why? What does this tell you about organizing a group for a task?
   - What one thing did you learn from this activity?

ROCK, PAPER, SCISSORS TRAIN

Energizers

Purpose: Provides an opportunity for everyone to get involved and be a winner.

Group Size: 50 – unlimited

Time: 5 – 10 minutes

Supplies: None, but if you have a large group, you'll need a large room.

Directions:

1. Make sure everyone understands the basics of the game "Rock, Paper, Scissors." A closed fist indicates "rock." A flat hand indicates "paper." The V for victory sign indicates "scissors." Two players each make three chopping motions with one of their arms and at the end of the third chop, they reveal which of the three options they chose by showing a fist, a flat hand, or a V sign. The winner is assessed as follows: Rock crushes scissors. Scissors cuts paper. Paper covers rock.

2. Have everyone find a partner.

3. Explain that when you say, "Go," each pair does a "RPS" game. Whoever loses puts their hands on the shoulders of the winner and starts a "train."

4. That train of two players then pairs with another two-person train.

5. Again, when you say, "Go," the two train leaders play "RPS." The losing train joins the winning train and forms a four-person train. The four-person trains pair with other four-person trains, and this pattern continues until there are just two long trains left.

6. Make a big deal about the final round between the two last "RPS" trains. The excitement of the team that wins is overwhelming. Even though at some point, mostly everyone "lost" the game, they end up rooting for their new team. We all love to be part of a winning team!

7. Have the team that loses the last round join the winning team and let the train do a victory lap. Play "The Locomotion" or some other fun music and just enjoy.

8. Most groups want to do this activity repeatedly.

ROPE WRITING

Purpose: Emphasizes team cooperation.

Group Size: 8 – 20

Time: 15 minutes

Supplies: 40 - 50 feet of rope or twine; blindfolds (or have everyone close their eyes).

Directions:

1. After making sure that everyone is blindfolded, hand each person a section of the rope, making sure everyone is equidistant from one another.

2. Explain that the group is to form a shape, letter, or short word that you call out. They are not to drop their section of the rope. When the group thinks they are done, one person in the group can let go of the rope and, still blindfolded, can feel his or her way around it and instruct the group how to adjust themselves if necessary to make their shape more accurate.

3. When the first shape is complete, have the group assess how they did and what would improve their performance. Then call out a new shape and see how the group works together this time.

4. Discuss the idea of cooperation and teamwork. Two good points:
   - Sometimes you have to trust that the other group members are doing their job even if you don't see them doing the work.
   - Everyone in a group must do their best even if no one is watching.

Variation

Do the activity in the same way but this time, instead of the blindfolds, tell the group that they cannot talk with one another. They have to use non-verbal communication. Ask them how not being able to talk helps or hinders the job. Discuss other ways that we communicate.

RUMORS

Purpose: Demonstrates how communication can get distorted and rumors start and spread.

Group Size: 10 – 30

Time: 15 minutes

Supplies: A copy of the Rumors worksheet (see Appendix page 92) and a pen or pencil for each participant.

Directions:

1. Have five people leave the room. Tell them they will come back individually to hear a story later. That's all they need to know.

2. Select two players to play the roles of Ben and Sue. Give them each a copy of the script and have them read their parts out loud. Tell the rest of the group to listen carefully to the story.

3. When the story is finished, have one of the five people who are outside of the room come back. Select one person who listened to the story to tell it to the person who just returned to the room. The storyteller should include as much detail as possible.

4. Tell the person who just returned to listen carefully to the details of the story.

5. Give the rest of the people in the room a copy of the story and tell them to read the story silently as the storyteller is speaking and to pay careful attention to the parts being left out.

6. The person who was just told the story now becomes the storyteller, and he or she must relate the story to the next person brought back into the room. This pattern continues until all five people have heard the story.

7. The last person to hear the story then relates it to the whole group.

8. Next, have Ben and Sue reread the original script.

9. Process the activity.
   - How did the story change as it was repeated?
   - What were some of the main details that were left out?
   - Is this story typical of something you might overhear? Why?
   - Did anyone add details that were not in the original story? Do people you know ever do that? Why?
   - How can you relate this to gossip and rumors in your school, group of friends, or work place?
   - If you hear rumors, what's the appropriate thing to do? How do you avoid getting into a situation like this?
   - Why is it hard to remember all the details?
   - Has any rumor ever circulated about you? How did you feel about that?

Note: Remind the group that the distortions that developed during this activity were not the fault of the people who left the room. Everyone just needs to remember the human tendency to forget details and to be sure to learn the real story before repeating any details.

SHUT EYE DRAWINGS

Purpose: Prompts discussion about seeing the big picture and making assumptions about ourselves and our lives. It also produces some funny artwork.

Group Size: Unlimited

Time: 10 minutes

Supplies: Paper and pencil for each person.

Directions:

1. Tell everyone that they are going to draw a picture and you will tell them what to draw.

2. Instruct participants to close their eyes and *keep them closed* while they are drawing.

3. Use the following list for things to draw. Make sure you read them in order and allow enough time in between items for the participants to draw each thing.

   a) the outline of a house   e) a door on the house

   b) a big tree next to the house   f) sun in the sky

   c) windows in the house   g) two birds in the nest

   d) a nest in the tree   h) chimney on the house

4. It adds to the fun if you ham it up when you mention each new item. Pretend that you don't realize that you're making everyone go back and forth to different parts of their pictures. There are lots of moans and groans when they have to find the right place to add the next item.

5. When you are finished with the list, tell everyone to open their eyes and look at their masterpieces. There will be lots of giggles.

6. Have everyone hold up their artwork for all to see.

7. Process the activity with the following analogy: Sometimes it's hard to get our lives right if we can't see the big picture. Just like in our drawings, things were out of place and less than perfect because we couldn't see what we were drawing. But if we can open our eyes to the situations and happenings around us, we can see our way more clearly and can make the necessary adjustments before our lives get too fragmented or off track.

   • What can make your life seem fragmented?

   • What or who helps you see the bigger picture?

   • What assumptions do we make about the lives of others?

   • How can we help one another get on the right track?

SKITTERGORIES

Purpose: A large group activity that gets people mixing with one another quickly.

Group Size: 50 – 125

Time: 20 – 30 minutes

Supplies: An index card (or slip of paper) for each person.

Directions:

1. Prepare by writing one item from a specific category on each card. (See suggestions below.) The number of items in a category should correspond to the number of participants you want in each group. Seven to ten is usually a good choice.

2. Give all group members a card and instruct them to keep them to themselves until everyone has one.

3. When you say "Go," they are to try to find all the other people who fit into their category. Their group then becomes a team.

4. After everyone has found their group, read the category lists aloud to be sure someone is not on the wrong team.

5. Give each team seven minutes to prepare a short skit that relates their category and each item in their category to whatever theme you choose—leadership, youth ministry, service, reaching out to others, and so forth.

6. Have each team present their skit for the whole group.

States	Trees	Colors
Colorado	pine	blue
Wisconsin	spruce	aqua
Alabama	elm	red
Rhode Island	maple	orange
Montana	birch	purple
Texas	oak	yellow
West Virginia	walnut	brown
Oklahoma	aspen	green

Sports	Flowers	Holidays
baseball	rose	Easter
basketball	zinnia	Ground Hog Day
football	carnation	St. Patrick's Day
soccer	daisy	Christmas
volleyball	aster	Thanksgiving
golf	marigold	Valentine's Day
gymnastics	tulip	Hanukkah
track	lily	Halloween

Other good categories include candy bars, cereal, brands of jeans, cheeses, song titles, vehicles, and tourist attractions.

SOUND OFF

Purpose: Invites people to step out of their comfort zones a little but provides lots of fun. It's best played with a group who knows one another at least a little.

Group Size: 10 – 20

Time: 5 – 10 minutes

Supplies: None

Directions:

1. Direct the group to sit in a circle.
2. Tell everyone that no one is to laugh during this activity. Anyone who laughs is out of the game. The last person to remain in the circle is the winner.
3. Going counter clockwise, have the person on your right start the game by passing a sound of some kind—a sniff, a snort, a hiccup, a squeal— to the person on his or her right. That person passes the sound along to the next person, and it continues all around the circle. If anyone laughs at any time, that person is out of the game.
4. When it gets back to you, pass the sound to the next person in line and that round is over.
5. Then have the second person in the circle make a new sound, and pass it to the person on his or her right. Continue until it gets back to you and you pass it on to the person on your right. That round is over, and you get a third round started.
6. Continue until all but one person is eliminated.

Note: The sound maker may add facial expressions, and the group must copy those as well as the sound.

TEAMWORK—LOGOS

Purpose: Offers a fun way to see the value of cooperation. The group is divided into small teams and everyone participates.

Group Size: Unlimited, in groups of 4 - 5 people each

Time: 10 minutes

Supplies: Each team needs a logo sheet (see Directions) and a pen or pencil.

Directions:

1. Make a logo sheet by cutting out recognizable letterhead or logos from well known companies or events. Paste them on a sheet of paper and leave a space to write. Make a copy for each participant.
2. When the group gathers, break them into teams, and distribute the logo sheets. Allow five to ten minutes for them to get as many answers as they can.
3. The group with the most correct answers is the winner.

Variation

Use this kind of activity as part of a treasure hunt. After hiding the treasures, use the logo letters to spell out clues to the locations of the treasure. For instance, if you have the logos for Nike, Coca Cola, Adidas, and Microsoft, you can cut apart the letters you need to spell DESK or FLOOR or FOLDER.

UP IN THE AIR!

Purpose: Provides a very lively activity that serves as a good springboard for discussion about juggling responsibilities in life.

Group Size: 10 – 30

Time: 15 minutes

Supplies: One balloon for each person, plus 10 additional balloons.

Directions:

1. Distribute one balloon to each person and have everyone blow up their balloon.

2. Explain that the goal of the game is to keep all the balloons in the air for as long as the group can manage it.

3. Point out that a penalty occurs when a balloon touches the floor, or if a balloon is left on the floor longer than five seconds after it falls. You will call out a penalty as it happens. The group is disqualified after accruing five penalties.

4. Start the action by saying, "Go."

5. Every ten seconds, add a balloon to those already in the air.

6. When the five penalties are reached, stop the activity, tell the group how long they kept the balloons in the air, and ask them to discuss how they could break their record. After a short discussion, have them try it again.

7. Process the activity.

   • What was your goal? Did you accomplish it?

   • Did you break your record with the second try? Why?

   • How did you feel when more balloons were being added to those already in the air?

   • Did you come up with a strategy to deal with the extras?

   • What are some responsibilities in your life?

   • What are some ways you juggle all the responsibilities in your life?

WACKY OLYMPICS

Purpose: A collection of activities done in teams. Can be separate events or can run concurrently during one big event.

Group Size: 10 – 25 per team

Time: Each game should be set for 3 - 5 minutes; a competition of 10 games with up to 10 teams takes about 45 minutes. As one team completes one event, another team can be working on a different event. Keep the teams moving from one event to the next.

Supplies: As listed for each game.

Alphabet Dancing

The team begins at the starting line. Three players run to a spot fifteen feet away, lie on the floor and form the letter *A* with their bodies. All three people have to be part of the letter. After you approve of their formation, they run back to the starting line, and the next three people run down to the spot and make the letter *B*. Keep going through the alphabet (and start over if you have to) until time is up. Give one point for each letter made.

Balloon Pop

Arrange team members in pairs and have them line up behind a starting line. Have a supply of uninflated balloons about twenty feet away from the starting line. (Eleven-inch balloons work well.) When you give the signal to start, the first pair must run to the balloons, blow one up, tie it, and then pop it by bumping it between their bodies. Once the balloon pops, they run back to the starting line, and the next pair goes. Give one point for each popped balloon.

Basketball Bounce

Put a large garbage can or box about seven feet from the starting line but don't have it tight against a wall. Each player takes a turn trying to bounce the basketball into the box or can. Players retrieve their own basketballs and bring them back to the starting line for the next player. Give one point for each ball that stays in the garbage can or box.

Bucket Pass

Have everyone lie on their backs in a circle, heads toward the middle of the circle and feet are in the air. They must pass a five-quart ice cream bucket or a three-pound coffee can around the circle using only their feet. Give one point for each person who successfully passes the bucket. Continue until time is up.

Chariot Race

This time the team works in groups of three. Don't worry if it doesn't work out to be even groups. Participants just match up as their turn comes. You need a strong blanket as the chariot. The object is for one person to ride on the chariot (blanket) while the other two pull him or her to the line fifteen feet away. At the line, one of the pullers hops on the chariot, the rider becomes a puller, and they pull the rider back to the start line. Keep this up until time is called. Give one point for each successful trip.

WACKY OLYMPICS (cont'd)

Cup Blow

Attach a string going through a styrofoam cup to two chairs. The distance between the two chairs should be about five feet. The object is to blow the cup from one chair to the other. The person should be blowing into the cup, not onto the back side of the cup. Participants will have to stoop or get down on their knees to be at cup level. Push the cup back to the starting spot when the blower gets it to the other chair. Give one point for each person who completes the task.

Frisbee Toss

Make a two-foot by two-foot square on the wall with masking tape. Make a line on the floor with tape about ten feet away from the square. The object is to throw the frisbee so it hits the wall inside of the square. Give one point for each hit in the square. (Experiment with the distance. You may have to adjust it for different age groups.)

Hula Hoop Relay

Put a hula hoop over one person's arm, then have the team hold hands. The object is to move the hula hoop from player to player without letting go of any hands. Count one point for each person the hoop passes over. Continue until time limit is up.

Over and Under

Line the team up in a straight line, everyone facing one direction (looking at the back of the head of the person in front of them). The first person is given a ball (a basketball, soccer ball, or volley-ball works well). The team's job is to pass the ball over their heads and between their legs in an alternating sequence. Thus, the first person passes the ball over his or her head, the second person passes the ball between his or her legs, the third person, over the head, the fourth person, between the legs, and so on. When the last person is reached, the ball is tossed up to the front person and they start again (but this time must start the opposite way they started the ball last time). Give one point for each person who handles the ball.

Plunger Run

Buy two plungers, take the head off one of them, and attach it to the end of the other plunger's stick, thus making a two-sided plunger. Arrange the team in pairs. The first two people position the plunger so that one end of it is on one person's belly and the other end of it is on the other person's belly. They must use their body force to keep the plunger between them. They can't touch the plunger. It works well if they put their hands on each other's shoulders. They must run from the starting line, around a chair or cone twenty feet away, and then back to the starting line. Then the next pair goes. Give one point for each pair who crosses the finish line.

Potato Squat

You need a few large potatoes and a low box for this game. Each player takes a turn. At the starting line the player puts a potato between his or her knees. The player must hop/walk/run to the box (about ten feet away) and drop the potato into the box. Once it falls in the player should grab it out of the box and run back to the starting line. Then the next person goes. Give one point for each potato dropped into the box.

Sponge Water Relay

The goal is to fill the team's bucket with more water than any other team's bucket. You need one sponge, a large five-gallon pail, at least one ice cream bucket and something with which to measure the water. The first person on the team dips the sponge into the five-gallon pail, which is already filled with water. The person runs fifteen feet to the ice cream bucket, squeezes out the sponge, runs back and passes the sponge to the next player. Measure each team's water amount after the time is up. The winner is the team with the most water. Points can be given for each teaspoon, cup, milliliter, or whatever your container measures in.

Spooning

You need one spoon and a few cotton balls for this game. The object is to carry the cotton ball from the starting line, down around a chair about ten feet away, and then back to the starting line. When the first person completes that, they hand off the spoon to the next person. Use very light cotton balls. They are a bit harder to maneuver when you're traveling at top speed. Give one point for each successful trip.

Stepping Stones

The group works in pairs in this game. One person in the pair is given two paper plates. These are the stepping stones on which the other person has to cross the murky swamp. Person A sets down a paper plate, and Person B can put one foot on it. A sets the next plate down so B can step on that. Person A keeps alternating plates until Person B gets to the finish line, which is about ten feet away. Then they trade places, and B lays down the plates while A is the stepper. Give one point for each successful trip.

Straw Drop (or Clothes Pin Drop)

For this activity, you need about twenty straws and a container with a somewhat narrow neck. Taking turns, each person takes a straw, holds it to their forehead, and tries to drop the straw into the container. They retrieve their straw from the container on the floor, and go back to the end of the line. You should keep a count of the straws that make it into the container and give one point for each straw. Substitute clothes pins for straws for a variation.

Tummy Tummy Ball

This is similar to the plunger game. This time each pair puts a basketball between their tummys, runs around the cone which is set about twenty feet away, and runs back to the starting line. Then the next pair goes. If the ball is dropped, the players can just pick it up where they're at and keep going. Give one point for each successful crossing.

Wacky Javelin

For this game you need one hula hoop and two or three foam pool noodles, available at all stores selling pool toys. Frisbees can be used also. One of the team members is the hula hoop holder. The holder stands about ten feet from the starting line. The other team members take turns throwing the wacky javelin (a foam pool noodle) into the hoop. The hoop holder may move the hoop around to try to get the javelin through. The thrower retrieves his or her own javelin. Give one point for each time a javelin goes through the hoop. (You can attach a small beanbag animal to the end of the javelins with duct tape to help them fly better.)

Energizers

WHEN SOMEONE CLAPS TWICE...

Purpose: Provides an excellent exercise in working together. If anyone isn't paying attention, the result is a total breakdown in the activity.

Group Size: 10 – 30

Time: 5 minutes, plus discussion time at your discretion

Supplies: Slips of paper with directions (see Appendix page 96); one piece of candy per person.

Directions:

1. Cut the page of directions into individual slips. Give one slip to each person. There are twenty-seven directions in this activity. It is important that each participant have at least one. If you have more than twenty-seven people, you will need to create more directions and slips. If you have fewer than twenty-seven people, you can give some people more than one slip.

2. Explain that everyone must work together to reach the goal. If everyone follows the direction on the slip they have, there will be a surprise at the end.

3. Then clap twice to get the game going.

4. Watch the progression. Usually, the activity will run through to the end smoothly. If it gets stopped somewhere in the middle, you have to decide if you want to try to keep the game moving along or just let it stop where communication breaks down. Processing the activity is interesting whether the game gets completed or gets bogged down.

5. When the activity is complete or stops because of lack of communication, take time to discuss it.

   - How did you feel as the activity went along?
   - What did you notice about group members during the activity?
   - What kind of situations can you relate this to in everyday life?
   - [If applicable] How did you feel about not completing it? How did you feel if you didn't get to do what was on your slip?
   - What aspects are important in setting and achieving goals?

WHO'S IN CHARGE?

Purpose: Highlights imagination and cooperation.

Group Size: 15 – 40

Time: 10 minutes

Supplies: None

Directions:

1. Have the group stand in a circle.
2. Ask one person to leave the room.
3. Tell the group to select someone to be in charge of the group. That person is to lead the group through various motions after the person outside the room returns. Some motions could be scratching the nose, winking, turning the head left or right, and so on. The leader can decide what motions to use.
4. The returning person is to try to figure out who is leading the group.
5. Explain that this will take a lot of strategy because it is hard not to look directly at the person in charge, which would give away the game very quickly.
6. After the first person figures out who the leader is and names the right person, another person leaves the room, and a new person is selected to be in charge.
7. See which leader can stay in charge the longest.

YES – NO – BLUE – BLACK

Purpose: Gets people talking to one another.

Group Size: Unlimited

Time: 10 minutes

Supplies: 5 tokens or counters for each person in the group (beans, pennies, or stones work well as counters).

Directions:

1. Give each person five tokens to begin the game.

2. Tell everyone they must mingle and talk with other group members. They are to try to win as many tokens from the others as possible. Tokens are won by getting someone to say *Yes, No, Blue,* or *Black.* If someone says any of those words, that person must give a token to whomever they are talking. (The homonyms *know* and *bleu* count!)

3. If a person runs out of tokens, that person can keep playing and try to win back some tokens, but he or she won't have any to give away until after winning some back.

4. The winner is the one with the most tokens after the time is up. Give an incredible prize to the one with the most tokens.

Do you like spinach?

What's the color of the sky on a sunny day?

Would you like to win the lottery?

How would you describe a panther?

BOUNDARY BREAKING QUESTIONS

- What are you most looking forward to in the next three months?
- What one thing do you want to be remembered for?
- What is one talent you would like to possess?
- What article of clothing that is worn by your mom or dad embarrasses you the most?
- What is your greatest accomplishment?
- If you had a crystal ball and could see the future, what one thing would you want to find out?
- Name one of your pet peeves.
- When you go back to school in the fall, what one thing do you hope to accomplish?
- What do you think is the hardest thing about dating?
- If your phone had a picture screen, how would your telephone habits change?
- Share something about your family that you are proud of.
- If you could travel to any place in time, when and where would you go?
- What is the best movie that you have ever seen?
- What's the best concert you've ever been to?
- What do you want to be doing ten years from now?
- Finish this statement: "The best thing about today is…."
- What kind of store would you like to own and operate?
- If you could have dinner with anyone, living or dead, who would it be?
- What person has most influenced your life?
- What is the best compliment you have received?
- If you could travel to any place in the world, where would you go first?
- What future discovery are you looking forward to the most?
- Name three things for which you are thankful.
- Select a word that best describes your life at this time.
- What would you like to invent to make life easier?
- Tell about the greatest Christmas present you have ever given/received.
- What emotion is strongest in you?
- What makes you laugh?
- How do you like to spend your free time?
- In your opinion, what profession benefits society the most?
- Name a goal you have set and reached.
- What makes a house a home?
- If you could change your age, what age would you be?
- If you had three wishes, what would you wish for?
- What is the best/last book you have read?
- What is your favorite television program?
- Describe your room.
- What is your favorite holiday?
- Do you think the world will be a better or worse place 100 years from now?
- If each day had six more hours, how would you spend them?
- What would constitute a perfect evening for you?

Appendix

BOUNDARY BREAKING QUESTIONS (cont'd)

- Would you rather get $10,000 for yourself or $100,000 to give away?
- What is your favorite quote?
- What subject is most frequently discussed among your friends?
- What one day in your life would you like to live over?
- What is your least favorite TV commercial?
- What event in your life has been a turning point for you?
- What do you miss the most about your childhood?
- Besides your parents, whom do you most admire?
- If you were going to write a TV show about yourself, what type would you write—soap, comedy, romance, drama? Why?
- Do you believe in angels/miracles?
- What one characteristic do you see in yourself that you also see in your parents/grandparents?
- In your opinion, what is the most pressing problem in the world today?
- When you feel sad/angry, what do you do to express yourself? What do you do to feel cheerful again?
- What is your favorite way to spend an evening with your parents?
- Of the five senses—sight, smell, touch, taste and hearing—which could you live without and which couldn't you bear to lose?
- How important is money to you?
- Would you tell the truth no matter what? When would you ever lie?
- If you were a fly on the wall, who would you want to eavesdrop on?
- What one thing would you place in a time capsule that would be discovered by future generations?
- What is your passion/purpose in life?
- If your house was burning, what three possessions would you save?
- If you could offer one piece of advice to your parents, what would it be?
- What day are you looking forward to the most?
- What is the most beautiful thing you have ever seen?
- When do you feel most productive?
- Complete this sentence: I hope….
- Describe your best phone call ever.
- If you could trade places with someone, who would it be?
- What, if anything, is too serious to be joked about?
- Describe your feelings about God—yourself—love—religion.
- Do you consider yourself a leader? Why or why not?
- When do you feel most lonely?
- Describe the person you would like to spend the rest of your life with.
- What is the most spiritual event you've ever experienced?
- What do you think people like in you the most/least?
- What is your most treasured memory?
- What is your most important goal now?
- What should you do that you have put off doing?
- Is there anything else you would like the group to know about you?

Appendix

GOTCHA!

Do everything on this list and get signatures to prove it. No duplicate signatures please!

1. Untie someone's shoe, then tie it again.

   Have the person sign here _____

2. Count out loud (as loud as you can) as you do ten jumping jacks with a partner.

   Have your partner sign here _____

3. Find someone who is left-handed.

   Have him or her sign here with the RIGHT hand _____

4. Have someone ELSE do 5 push-ups for you.

   Have the person sign here _____

5. Get someone to sing a TV commercial and sign here _____

6. Do your very best impersonation of a cow, pig, or chicken for someone.

   Ask the person to sign here _____

7. Find someone whose birthday is in the same month as yours and ask the person to sign with both his or her name and month of birth.

   Name _____ Birth Month _____

8. Get six different autographs and each person's place of birth on the back of this sheet.

9. Find someone whose eyes are a different color than yours.

   Ask the person to sign here _____

10. Get four other people to form a circle with you and sing one verse of "Row, Row, Row Your Boat."
    Have the four people sign the back of this sheet.

11. Ask someone to give you a penny and to sign here _____

12. Find six people and have a group hug!

HOW MANY SQUARES?

I CAN FIND THAT!

This is a game of searching, noticing, and finding. Here is a list of items you and your group members need to find and check off the list. Please write down where the item was found. All items are in this room. All are in plain view. You do not have to move anything to find these items. When you find an item, leave it where it is, and play it cool. Good Luck!

Item	Where Found

1. large paper clip _____

2. match _____

3. ruler _____

4. paper airplane _____

5. sunglasses _____

6. eraser _____

7. shiny confetti _____

8. penny _____

9. kazoo _____

10. balloon _____

11. lipstick container _____

12. rubber band _____

13. band-aid _____

14. aspirin_____

15. button _____

16. spool of thread _____

17. key _____

18. postage stamp_____

19. thumbtack_____

20. nail _____

"IT GIVES ME GREAT PLEASURE TO INTRODUCE..."

Our special guest today is [Name]_____ .

As you all know, [he or she] is widely known and highly acclaimed for [special accomplishments] _____

_____

[Name] has spent a great deal of time learning to _____ ,

and recently demonstrated [his or her] powers of persuasion by convincing _____

to _____ .

Our guest says [he or she] stays active by _____

and _____ .

You may have read that [name] recently added_____

and _____to [his or her] material possessions, and is planning to add

_____ in the near future.

One of the most enjoyable pastimes for [Name] is _____ .

You can surely see that [Name]_____ is a remarkable person.

It gives me great pleasure to introduce [Name].

PEOPLE BINGO

B	I	N	G	O
Can juggle	Saw a live concert in the past year	Plays a fall sport	Wears the same size shoe as you do	Will sing "Row, Row, Row Your Boat" for you
Has been to the movies in the last 2 weeks (What did they see?)	Read 3 or more books in the past 3 months	Hates to mow the lawn	Has been in a drama production	Has a computer at home
Worked a part time job this summer	Favorite food is pizza	Has a birthday in the same month as you	Can tell you what CPR stands for	Went to 3 or more baseball games this summer
Can do a cartwheel	Knows a clean joke	Has brown eyes	Reads "Peanuts" or "Beetle Bailey"	Watches "Days of our Lives" or "General Hospital"

Appendix

PERSONAL CREST

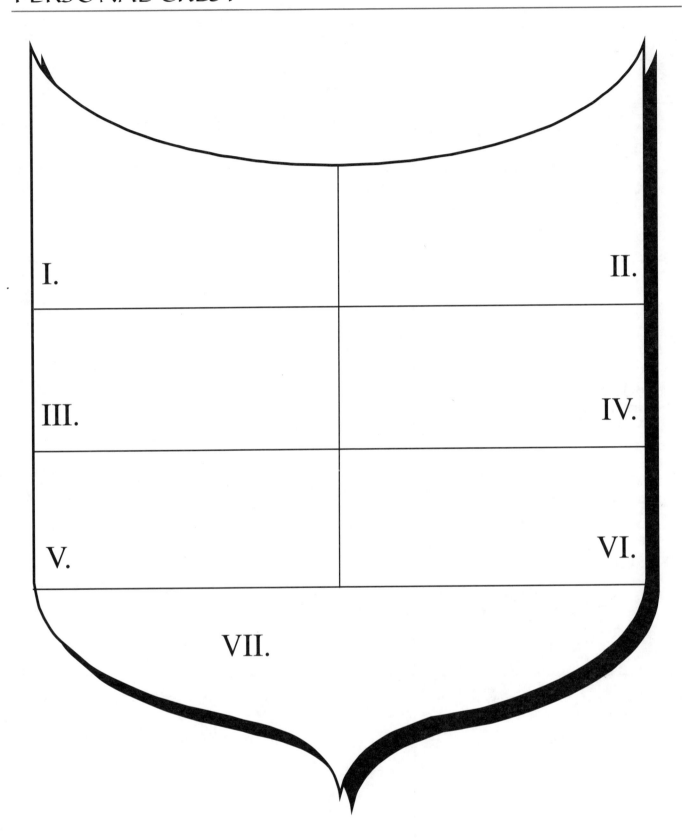

I.

II.

III.

IV.

V.

VI.

VII.

Appendix

PICTURE PROVERBS

Don't cry over spilt milk.
One who laughs last laughs best.
A bird in the hand is worth two in the bush.
A stitch in time saves nine.
Don't put the cart before the horse.
Money is the root of all evil.
Too many cooks spoil the broth.
Look before you leap.
The early bird catches the worm.
Steady wins the race.
Hear no evil, see no evil, speak no evil.
You will be judged by the company you keep.
Good things come in small packages.
Do as I say, not as I do.
Think before you speak.
Absence makes the heart grow fonder.
Out of sight, out of mind.
Every cloud has a silver lining.
A chain is only as strong as its weakest link.
Laugh, and the world laughs with you; cry, and you cry alone.
Pride comes before a fall.
Beauty is in the eye of the beholder.
To err is human, to forgive, divine.
Monkey see, monkey do.
People who live in glass houses shouldn't throw stones.

RUMORS

The Story

Sue: What did you do this weekend, Ben?

Ben: Well, it wasn't too exciting. On Saturday, a bunch of us hung out at the mall since it was raining. What'd you do?

Sue: Well, we were supposed to have a softball game at noon on Saturday, and even though it was raining lightly, we were all out there ready to play. Well, then it turns out that the other team thought the game was canceled, so they never showed up. And I missed out on a camping trip with my cousin just to play in the stupid game.

Ben: It wasn't too exciting at the mall either. A bunch of us were going to go to a movie, but we couldn't decide what to see. Then Amy, Jennifer, and Kate showed up, and they were trying to convince us to go see "Lost in the Ozone." We didn't really want to see that, but you know how Mike sorta likes Amy, so he tried to convince her to come with us. Well, then the other two got mad. It was really a pain.

Sue: Boy! Then I guess I'm glad I wasn't there. Well, our coach ended up taking us to Pizza Place for lunch, which was really fun, but while we were eating, someone backed their car into his van. Then I had to call my parents to come pick me up because our coach had to wait for the police to come.

Ben: Well, maybe next weekend we can find something fun to do!

TALKING BUDDIES

- If you could have lived in a different time in history, when would it have been and why?

- What is something you are proud of that you have worked hard for?

- If a crystal ball could tell you the truth about any one thing you wished to know about your future, what would you want to know?

- If you could wake up tomorrow having gained one ability or quality, what would it be?

- What would constitute a "perfect evening" for you?

- Your house, containing everything you own, catches fire. After saving your loved ones and pets, you have time to safely make a final dash to save any item. What would it be? What makes it so significant?

- If you could interview any person who has ever lived, who would it be and why?

- What world event so far in your life has affected you the most? How?

- What would you like to be doing in ten years?

- What do you admire the most about your best friend?

Appendix

THIS IS ME!

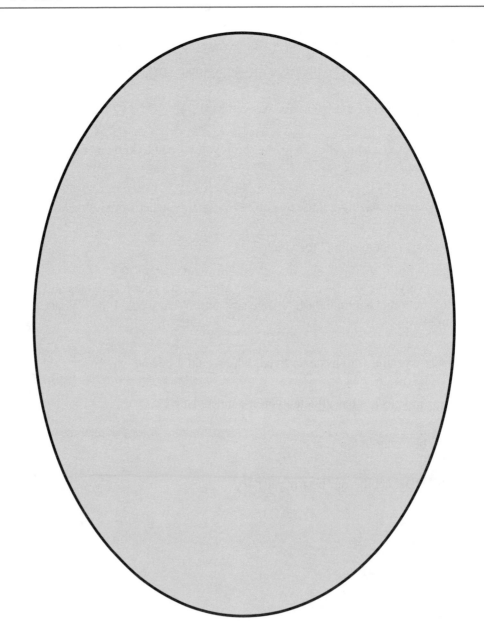

Who Drew This?

Left eye _____

Right eye _____

Left ear_____

Nose _____

Hair _____

Right ear _____

Mouth_____

Right eyebrow _____

Left eyebrow _____

TWELVE SQUARES

Appendix

WHEN SOMEONE CLAPS TWICE...

When someone claps twice, stand up and say, "Good Morning."
When someone says, "Good Morning," get up and turn off the lights.
When someone turns off the lights, clap once and yell, "It's dark in here."
When someone yells, "It's dark in here," get up and turn on the lights.
When someone turns on the lights, stand up and spin around twice.
When someone spins around twice, make a cow noise.
When someone makes a cow noise, stand up and say, "I'm glad to be here."
When someone says, "I'm glad to be here," whistle.
When someone whistles, stand up and flap your arms like a bird.
When someone flaps their arms like a bird, stand on your chair.
When someone stands on their chair, say, "Get down from there."
When someone says, "Get down from there," make a loud sneezing sound.
When someone makes a loud sneezing sound, feel the forehead of the person next to you and shout, "Someone get a doctor."
When someone shouts, "Someone get a doctor," sing, "I'm a Little Teapot."
When someone sings, "I'm a Little Teapot," walk around the group leader three times.
When someone walks around the group leader three times, laugh really loud.
When someone laughs really loud, stomp your feet.
When someone stomps their feet, do a cheerleading move or jump.
When someone does a cheerleading move or jump, tell us what time it is.
When someone tells us what time it is, shake hands and introduce yourself to the tallest male in the room.
When someone introduces themselves to the tallest male in the room, say, "I have a question."
When someone says, "I have a question," say, "I have an answer."
When someone says, "I have an answer," come to the front of the room and make the letter *Y* with your arms.
When someone makes the letter *Y* with their arms, choose two other people, come to the front of the room and make the letters *M*, *C*, and *A*.
When someone makes the letters *M*, *C*, and *A*, hop on one foot for five seconds.
When someone hops on one foot, say, "Here comes Peter Cottontail."
When someone says, "Here comes Peter Cottontail," give everyone a piece of candy.

Appendix